EMMANUE

Best known for his theories of ethics and responsibility, Emmanuel Levinas was one of the most profound and influential thinkers of the last century. Exploring the intellectual and social contexts of his work and the events that shaped it, Hand considers:

- the influence of phenomenology and Judaism on Levinas's thought
- key concepts such as the 'face', the 'other', ethical consciousness and responsibility
- Levinas's work on aesthetics
- the relationship of philosophy and religion in his writings
- the interaction of his work with historical discussions
- his often complex relationships with other theorists and theories

This outstanding guide to Levinas's work will prove invaluable to scholars and students across a wide range of disciplines – from philosophy and literary criticism through to international relations and the creative arts.

Seán Hand is Professor of French and Head of the Department of French Studies at the University of Warwick. His central research interests focus on twentieth-century French writing and philosophy.

ROUTLEDGE CRITICAL THINKERS

Series Editor: Robert Eaglestone, Royal Holloway, University of London

Routledge Critical Thinkers is a series of accessible introductions to key figures in contemporary critical thought.

With a unique focus on historical and intellectual contexts, the volumes in this series examine important theorists':

- significance
- motivation
- key ideas and their sources
- impact on other thinkers

Concluding with extensively annotated guides to further reading, *Routledge Critical Thinkers* are the student's passport to today's most exciting critical thought.

Already available:

For further information on this series, see www.routledge.com/literature/series.asp

EMMANUEL LEVINAS

Seán Hand

LONDON AND NEW YORK

First published 2009
by Routledge
2 Park Square, Milton Park, Abingdon, OX14 4RN

Simultaneously published in the USA and Canada
by Routledge
270 Madison Ave, New York, NY 10016

Routledge is an imprint of the Taylor & Francis Group, an informa business

© Seán Hand, 2009

Typeset in Perpetua by
Taylor & Francis Books
Printed and bound in Great Britain by
TJ International Ltd, Padstow, Cornwall

British Library Cataloguing in Publication Data
A catalogue record for this book is available from the British Library

Library of Congress Cataloging in Publication Data
A catalog record for this book has been requested

ISBN 13: 978-0-415-40276-7 (hbk)
ISBN 13: 978-0-415-40275-0 (pbk)
ISBN 13: 978-0-203-88805-6 (ebk)

ISBN 10: 0-415-40276-X (hbk)
ISBN 10: 0-415-40275-1 (pbk)
ISBN 10: 0-203-88805-7 (ebk)

CONTENTS

SERIES EDITOR'S PREFACE

The books in this series offer introductions to major critical thinkers who have influenced literary studies and the humanities. The *Routledge Critical Thinkers* series provides the books you can turn to first when a new name or concept appears in your studies.

Each book will equip you to approach a key thinker's original texts by explaining their key ideas, putting them into context and, perhaps most importantly, showing you why this thinker is considered to be significant. The emphasis is on concise, clearly written guides which do not presuppose a specialist knowledge. Although the focus is on particular figures, the series stresses that no critical thinker ever existed in a vacuum but, instead, emerged from a broader intellectual, cultural and social history. Finally, these books will act as a bridge between you and the thinkers' original texts: not replacing them but rather complementing what they wrote. In some cases, volumes consider small clusters of thinkers, working in the same area, developing similar ideas or influencing each other.

These books are necessary for a number of reasons. In his 1997 autobiography, *Not Entitled*, the literary critic Frank Kermode wrote of a time in the 1960s:

> On beautiful summer lawns, young people lay together all night, recovering from their daytime exertions and listening to a troupe of Balinese musicians.

> Under their blankets or their sleeping bags, they would chat drowsily about the gurus of the time … What they repeated was largely hearsay; hence my lunchtime suggestion, quite impromptu, for a series of short, very cheap books offering authoritative but intelligible introductions to such figures.

There is still a need for 'authoritative but intelligible introductions'. But this series reflects a different world from the 1960s. New thinkers have emerged and the reputations of others have risen and fallen, as new research has developed. New methodologies and challenging ideas have spread through the arts and humanities. The study of literature is no longer – if it ever was – simply the study and evaluation of poems, novels and plays. It is also the study of ideas, issues and difficulties which arise in any literary text and in its interpretation. Other arts and humanities subjects have changed in analogous ways.

With these changes, new problems have emerged. The ideas and issues behind these radical changes in the humanities are often presented without reference to wider contexts or as theories which you can simply 'add on' to the texts you read. Certainly, there's nothing wrong with picking out selected ideas or using what comes to hand – indeed, some thinkers have argued that this is, in fact, all we can do. However, it is sometimes forgotten that each new idea comes from the pattern and development of somebody's thought and it is important to study the range and context of their ideas. Against theories 'floating in space', the *Routledge Critical Thinkers* series places key thinkers and their ideas firmly back in their contexts.

More than this, these books reflect the need to go back to the thinkers' own texts and ideas. Every interpretation of an idea, even the most seemingly innocent one, offers you its own 'spin', implicitly or explicitly. To read only books on a thinker, rather than texts by that thinker, is to deny yourself a chance of making up your own mind. Sometimes what makes a significant figure's work hard to approach is not so much its style or the content as the feeling of not knowing where to start. The purpose of these books is to give you a 'way in' by offering an accessible overview of these thinkers' ideas and works and by guiding your further reading, starting with each thinker's own texts. To use a metaphor from the philosopher Ludwig Wittgenstein (1889–1951), these books are ladders, to be thrown away after you have climbed to the next level. Not only, then, do they equip you to approach new ideas, but also they empower you, by leading you back to the theorist's own texts and encouraging you to develop your own informed opinions.

Finally, these books are necessary because, just as intellectual needs have changed, the education systems around the world – the contexts in which introductory books are usually read – have changed radically, too. What was suitable for the minority higher education systems of the 1960s is not suitable for the larger, wider, more diverse, high technology education systems of the twenty-first century. These changes call not just for new, up-to-date introductions but new methods of presentation. The presentational aspects of *Routledge Critical Thinkers* have been developed with today's students in mind.

Each book in the series has a similar structure. They begin with a section offering an overview of the life and ideas of the featured thinkers and explain why they are important. The central section of each book discusses the thinkers' key ideas, their context, evolution and reception; with the books that deal with more than one thinker, they also explain and explore the influence of each on each. The volumes conclude with a survey of the impact of the thinker or thinkers, outlining how their ideas have been taken up and developed by others. In addition, there is a detailed final section suggesting and describing books for further reading. This is not a 'tacked-on' section but an integral part of each volume. In the first part of this section you will find brief descriptions of the thinkers' key works, then, following this, information on the most useful critical works and, in some cases, on relevant websites. This section will guide you in your reading, enabling you to follow your interests and develop your own projects. Throughout each book, references are given in what is known as the Harvard system (the author and the date of a work cited are given in the text and you can look up the full details in the bibliography at the back). This offers a lot of information in very little space. The books also explain technical terms and use boxes to describe events or ideas in more detail, away from the main emphasis of the discussion. Boxes are also used at times to highlight definitions of terms frequently used or coined by a thinker. In this way, the boxes serve as a kind of glossary, easily identified when flicking through the book.

The thinkers in the series are 'critical' for three reasons. First, they are examined in the light of subjects which involve criticism: principally literary studies or English and cultural studies, but also other disciplines which rely on the criticism of books, ideas, theories and unquestioned assumptions. Second, they are critical because studying their work will provide you with a 'tool kit' for your own informed critical reading and thought, which will make you critical. Third, these thinkers are critical because they are crucially important: they deal with ideas and questions which can overturn conventional under-standings of the world, of texts, of everything we take for granted, leaving us with a deeper understanding of what we already knew and with new ideas.

No introduction can tell you everything. However, by offering a way into critical thinking, this series hopes to begin to engage you in an activity which is productive, constructive and potentially life-changing.

ACKNOWLEDGEMENTS

I am grateful to the Arts and Humanities Research Council for funding a period of research leave which enabled me to complete this book. I am equally thankful to the University of Warwick, and to the Department of French Studies, for granting me a matching period of leave. For permissions to draw on some material previously published, I am grateful to Professor Lawrence Schehr, editor of *Contemporary French Civilization*, 30(2) (2006), and to the publishers and the editor, Dr Benda Hofmeyr, of *Radical Passivity. Rethinking Ethical Agency in Levinas* (Dordrecht: Springer, 2008). Certain ideas presented here were first explored in papers given at the Universities of Florida and Warwick; at the Jan Van Eyck Academy, Maastricht; at the Dun Laoghaire Institute of Art, Design and Technology; and at the Institute of Germanic and Romance Studies, London: I thank the organizers for their invitations, and the audiences for their insights. I am very grateful to the series' general editor, Professor Robert Eaglestone, and to the Commissioning Editor, Polly Dodson, and the Editorial Assistant, Emma Nugent, both of Routledge Literature, and to Laura Palosuo, Production Editor for Taylor & Francis, for all their help in overseeing the progress of the manuscript. And as always, I am indebted absolutely to Maolíosa and Dominic.

ABBREVIATIONS

WORKS BY LEVINAS

CP	*Collected Philosophical Papers*
DEH	*Discovering Existence with Husserl*
DEHH	*En découvrant l'existence avec Husserl et Heidegger*
DF	*Difficult Freedom*
EE	*Existence and Existents*
EI	*Ethics and Infinity*
HO	*Humanism of the Other*
IRB	*Is it Righteous to Be?*
LR	*The Levinas Reader*
MHO	'Martin Heidegger and Ontology'
NTR	*Nine Talmudic Readings*
OB	*Otherwise than Being or Beyond Essence*
OE	*On Escape*
PN	*Proper Names*
RPH	'Reflections on the Philosophy of Hitlerism'
TI	*Totality and Infinity*
TIHP	*The Theory of Intuition in Husserl's Phenomenology*
TO	*Time and the Other*
UH	*Unforeseen History*
WO	'Wholly Otherwise'

OTHER WORKS

AEL	Jacques Derrida, *Adieu to Emmanuel Levinas*
AT	Jacques Derrida, 'At This Very Moment in This Work Here I Am'
C	Jean Halperin and Georges Levitte (eds), *La conscience juive face à la guerre. Données et débats*
E	Alain Badiou, *Ethics. An Essay on the Understanding of Evil*
EA	Judith Butler, 'Ethical Ambivalence'
EP	Jean-Luc Marion, *The Erotic Phenomenon*
HAP	Philippe Lacoue-Labarthe, *Heidegger, Art and Politics. The Fiction of the Political*
HH	Martin Heidegger, *Hölderlin's Hymn 'The Ister'*
IM	Martin Heidegger, *An Introduction to Metaphysics*
N	Slavoj Žižek, 'Neighbors and Other Monsters: A Plea for Ethical Violence'
OW	Martin Heidegger, 'The Origin of the Work of Art'
PL	Judith Butler, *Precarious Life. The Powers of Mourning and Violence*
SE	Seán Hand, 'Shadowing Ethics: Levinas's View of Art and Aesthetics'
SR	Franz Rosenzweig, *The Star of Redemption*
TDF	Tina Chanter, *Time, Death, and the Feminine. Levinas with Heidegger*
VN	Jean-Luc Marion, 'The Voice without Name: Homage to Levinas'
WD	Jacques Derrida, *Writing and Difference*
WOD	Maurice Blanchot, *The Writing of the Disaster*

WHY LEVINAS?

Why Emmanuel Levinas indeed? This Lithuanian-born philosopher (1906–95) presented an uncompromising ethics that was grounded in both a pure phenomenological training and a deep Judaic heritage. In an age of spectacular and populist theorizing, he seemed to represent an educational and social past. Born in an age of Empires, he was the director of a modest teacher-training school; a diligent if hardly famous teacher and administrator; a university professor whose career began very late; and an observant Jew who for most of his life had little recognition or status within the official Jewish community of France. As an ex-student of Husserl and Heidegger who was at least credited with introducing phenomenology into France by way of early explanation and translation, but whose major works could be linguistically and intellectually tortuous, he suffered often from the insinuation that it was others who had really developed and popularized these radical ideas. Moreover, in Levinas's later years, some of his assumed positions came to be criticized as Eurocentric, politically and socially conservative, and implicitly sexist. His involved and even obsessed philosophy also seemed too difficult in form and too subtle and agonizing in message for any excited and media-savvy commentary, relying as it did on a deep knowledge and re-examination of the canon of Western philosophy and literature, and the core texts of the Judaeo-Christian religious tradition, in order to produce a demanding lesson about an ethics beyond all ethics. In short, the old-fashioned mannerly phrase: 'After you', which Levinas used sometimes as a small illustration of moral vigilance, could be accepted quite literally by some more fashionable critical theorists.

By the time of Levinas's death, however, this same thinker had become widely recognized as key to a fundamental post-war development in Western thinking, and one of the most radical influences on a wide variety of disciplines, ranging beyond philosophy or textual criticism to embrace geopolitical relations, theology, psychiatry or the ethics of creativity. At his burial service, the philosopher Jacques Derrida described the work of Levinas as 'so large one can no longer glimpse its edges' (AEL 3), adding in a resonant phrase:

[o]ne can predict with confidence that centuries of readings will set this as their task. We already see innumerable signs ... that the reverberations of this thought will have changed the course of philosophical reflection in our time, and of our reflection *on* philosophy, on what orders it according to ethics, according to another thought of ethics, responsibility, justice, the State, etc., according to another thought of the other, a thought that is newer than so many novelties because it is ordered according to the absolute anteriority of the face of the Other.

(AEL 3–4)

As we shall see in the course of this book, a bringing-together of radicality and 'anteriority', or the founding of new modes of thinking on the basis of a responsibility that comes before all organization, is given to us by the very nature of Levinas's texts and the kind of activity they call forth from us. His references and subject matter are a deep, European, education in themselves. To read Levinas involves having to read and recognize the force of the Bible and Plato, Descartes and Shakespeare, Hegel and Kierkegaard, and Bergson and Proust. But far from using these references in a consolidating or complacent manner, Levinas's reformulations of such writers re-instate them as urgently relevant.

Levinas's evocations of tradition often involve subjecting tradition to demanding re-appraisal. Part of the force of this questioning in Levinas comes also from his interdisciplinary probings: advanced philosophical cross-examination; a deep cultural practice of exegesis represented by study of the Talmud; critical appreciation of literature and the visual arts; the historical and ethical experience of the Shoah; and uncompromising political and geopolitical perspectives on post-war developments all come together in a complete vision of ethical existence. In following his example, we are brought to question many of our core critical assumptions about the foundations and purpose of being, or the nature and worth of aesthetics, or gender representations, or economics and politics (none of these assumptions being merely contemporary, as Levinas quickly shows). A specific example of this critical re-evaluation is the challenging nature of Levinas's negative judgement on the limits and priorities of 'anti-humanist' theories, such as structuralism, which dominated critical developments in the sixties and seventies. At the heart of such revisions, where Levinas's writings over time can become more truly radical than many of the latest critical novelties because of their absolute primary and singular task of re-appraisal, we have the fundamental example of Levinas's trenchant and unrelenting exposure of the links between Heidegger's ontology of being and the submersion of freedom beneath a philosophy of force. The chilling lesson which Levinas produced for us here, without ever reducing the argument to this theme alone, concerns how an arrogant intellectual mastery of reality can help to produce the horror of Auschwitz.

Levinas's readings therefore always also sustain a necessary ethical practice of *un*reading, a practice which perpetually invokes us and challenges all our assumptions. Overall, then, Levinas's writings engage us in a deep reappraisal of key texts, movements and ideas in the Western traditions, as well as of their related criticism. The logic of this naturally extends well beyond the fields of phenomenology. Contemporary post-secular philosophy or post-modern theology, for example, has become radically renewed in recent years through reference to Levinas. Outside the worlds of academic or critical practice, Levinas's fundamental ethical message now also occupies a huge significance in guiding essential questions about democracy and secularism, state and security, asylum and rights, religion and rationalism, and he is now regularly appropriated for pointed debates about Zionism, post-9/11 political strategy, or notions of extremism. In sum, most if not all fields of ethical debate have been renewed and tested in recent years by the referencing of Levinas. We read him, therefore, not just as an exemplary inquiry into tumultuous ideas and politics of the twentieth century, but also as a superb example of perpetual critical practice, and as a fundamental and unending ethical lesson concerning the aims and ends of our being.

THIS BOOK

Given the breadth of interest in Levinas, it is all the more necessary to give a clear account of his writing that can be generally understood. This book's overall aim is to do just that, and it embeds this aim in its approach and the quite specific readings given in each chapter. Each of Levinas's major works is therefore discussed for its detailed ethical engagements with key positions, texts and thinkers, but also for some of its most pressing contextual significance. This includes both historical and intellectual circumstances, which, as we shall see, can therefore logically involve Levinas also having to revise some of his own previous books or positions. When ideas are broached, they are always located concretely in the text being discussed, as when we try to understand Levinas's concept of the face, or of substitution. The aim is to show how Levinas's practice of ever-revising ethics emerges cumulatively, and involves both logical and political and cultural development. This approach runs in tandem with a general attempt to demystify Levinas, since his ideas, references and even style are difficult enough, but also because his very difficulty tempts some writers to offer paraphrases of Levinas which can end up sounding even more difficult. I have therefore wanted always to ground Levinas's ideas and language in their historical and cultural specificity, but also to react critically where I believed that criticism was to me justified. Where key terms or names are first raised, I offer a brief description, contained in a box at the end of the same section. I also conclude each chapter with a simple summary. Finally, I adopt the practice throughout of quoting in English, while highlighting any linguistic ambiguities when necessary by referring also to the original text in French.

These general aims condition each of the chapters. Given the importance of momentous historical events to the evolution of Levinas's writing as well as the need to place him in a number of intricate contexts, relating to both phenomenological and Jewish strands of thought and discussion, the book opens with a biographical chapter. This chapter highlights significant personal details as well as some key dates and events, and indicates some of Levinas's most significant circumstances, intellectual developments, and institutional and political engagements.

This sets up closer readings in subsequent chapters, which look to draw out the main significance and purpose of Levinas's most important works, in an initially chronological manner. I first cover Levinas's intellectual and specifically phenomenological formation up to the Second World War, focusing on what he took from his famous teachers Husserl and Heidegger, looking at how his ideas and writing changed as he registered the rise of the Shoah and what he saw as a philosophical complicity in the political degeneration, and then noting the subsequent emergence in Levinas of a more independent phenomenological account of being which anticipated later ethical writings that flowered in the post-war period.

The next chapter therefore focuses on this post-war evolution, which culminated in the first major book of philosophy, the 1961 *Totality and Infinity*, where Levinas explicitly seeks to present a critique of Western ontology. I detail how the synthesizing of phenomena is rejected now in favour of a thought that is open to the other, and I locate this ethical development in the developed notion of the face.

After reviewing how Levinas suggests that the other before me exceeds any idea of the other, I turn in my next chapter to the second of Levinas's most famous texts, the 1974 *Otherwise than Being or Beyond Essence*. I emphasize how this work consciously revises aspects of *Totality and Infinity* as it seeks to move to a new form of philosophical and ethical writing. That is to say, Levinas's rejection of the impersonal idea of the other in favour of a primordial indebtedness to the other becomes applied by him to philosophy's own intellectualism, as still latent in his work. I therefore comment on what the implications of this development are for Levinas's own philosophical language and structure, before reviewing the new series of dramatic evocations which emerge, chief of these being the crucially important notion of substitution.

Having thus far followed a chronological path in order to bring out the evolution of key ideas, I then turn my attention to a number of cross-cutting areas in Levinas where, in a post-war climate of rapidly changing ideas and loyalties, his ethics encounters particular problems and constructs different responses. The first of these areas concerns the status and potential of the artwork. Though he published consistently on art and artists, Levinas's concern for a primary ethics, his traditional cultural wariness towards image-making, and his polemic with Heidegger for whom the artwork assumed special significance, led him often to criticize artworks severely, as a potential evasion of responsibility. I trace the multiple reasons for Levinas's suspicion of the artwork, before following the subtle development in his texts of a more positive if highly partial view of the artwork's potential. In the course of this chapter, I recall Levinas's presentation of writers such as Proust, Blanchot and Celan, as well as draw out the obvious references in Levinas to Heidegger's elevation of the artwork.

The next chapter then turns to the Talmudic readings which Levinas consistently produced from the late fifties on, often in the context of the annual colloquium of French-speaking Jewish intellectuals. I show how his recourse to this traditional form of exegesis permitted Levinas to anchor his philosophy in an established and yet potentially radical practice of reading based on perpetual ethical inquiry. As a result, Levinas was able to adhere loyally to a Jewish and largely European culture of inquiry while using both the affiliation and the specific readings themselves to undo certain 'Heideggerian' versions of the themes and dramas evoked. In the course of giving these readings, for reasons of timing and conference theme, Levinas also came to elide aspects of his philosophical world-view with a messianic view of Israel.

This context leads logically to my following chapter, where I examine a chronological development of certain political perspectives in Levinas, running from the repudiation of Heidegger in the thirties and forties, through what we could term Levinas's 'Cold War' essays of the fifties and sixties, and into a number of 'Zionist' readings and Talmudic commentaries in the seventies which attempted to re-formulate the politics of the State of Israel in ethical terms.

My book then concludes with an attempt to view the critical scene 'after Levinas' by focusing on a number of recent profound appreciations of Levinas. In different and even conflicting ways, the leading thinkers reviewed here collectively demonstrate for us the profound significance that Levinas's work has now assumed for many different disciplines, whether philosophy, theology, political analysis or feminism. Finally, an extended bibliography gives a summary of the contents of key books by and on Levinas, and adds an indication of how some of these might be of potential use for future critical thinking.

KEY IDEAS

1

BIOGRAPHY

KAUNAS

From the beginning, Emmanuel Levinas's life was affected by dramatic alternatives that had huge political as well as intellectual implications. He was born into a Jewish family in Lithuania, on 30 December 1905 according to the Julian calendar that was still used in that part of the world at this time, that is to say on 12 January 1906 in our contemporary Gregorian calendar. His home town in Lithuania was Kaunas, which at that time was still part of the Russian Empire. It was therefore known also as Kovno to Russian speakers and as Kovne to many Jewish inhabitants, who formed roughly a third of the local population. Daily life was often rather traditionally sectarianized, with Russians generally administering authority, Lithuanians running agricultural production and Jews engaged in commerce. His family were rather middle-class but still observantly Jewish, and as his father ran a bookshop that catered for local government officials and the grammar school, there was daily contact with non-Jewish clients.

The Jews of Lithuania (or 'Litvaks' as they were sometimes termed) were generally *mitnagdim*, or 'opponents' of a mystical approach to religion, subscribing instead to a more sober, intellectual Judaism that placed a high value on education and study. Russian-language culture dominated this world of educational improvement with imperial force: Levinas's mother apparently could recite by heart one of the founding classics of modern Russian literature, *Eugene Onegin*, by the Romantic poet Pushkin, while Jewish parents looking to the future would often speak Russian to their children. But German was also publicly present (including via Yiddish), and Hebrew was studied in a traditional manner by the young Levinas, as part of a standard religious upbringing. It is worth bearing in mind, then, that the French language of his philosophy was a fourth form of communication, which he perfected only during his student years.

At the same time, Levinas was born on the cusp of revolutionary change. While he could later recall hearing about the death of the nineteenth-century literary giant Tolstoy, in 1910, or the tri-centennial celebrations of the last imperial dynasty of Russia, the House of Romanov, he was also fundamentally a child of the 1905 Russian revolution, which the revolutionary leader Trotsky was to describe as a 'revolutionary prologue'. In 1915, when Kaunas was taken by the Germans during the First World War, Levinas's family fled to Karkhov, in the Ukraine, where he moved to a non-Jewish secondary school (to which five Jews maximum were permitted entry). However, the 1917 October Revolution then created dangerous conditions for the family there, leading them in 1920 to flee back to Kaunas, which became in that year the temporary capital of a newly independent Lithuania. It was from here that Levinas eventually graduated from a Jewish secondary school. Our first picture of Levinas, then, is of an intellectually gifted, multi-lingual, Jewish boy whose early experiences of world war, proletarian revolution, precarious belonging and persecution were filtered through the particular circumstances and priorities of Jewish life inside a changing Lithuania. This initial experience of extreme events, mediated and transformed by intellect and endurance, would undoubtedly influence Levinas's eventual philosophical vision.

STRASBOURG

It was educational ambition and the freedom which it represented that led Levinas out of Lithuania. He eventually opted to study at the University of Strasbourg, arriving in 1923. Along with the rest of Alsace, this city had been returned to France from Germany at the end of the First World War, and its university was now consciously engaged in reasserting 'French' ideas, with the help of an ambitious new generation of scholars, whose generally republican and avant-garde tendencies somewhat set them apart from the surrounding region's Christian conservatism.

Levinas studied philosophy under a number of respected teachers who left their mark in small but telling ways. One such was Maurice Pradines, who had strikingly illustrated the purpose of ethics to Levinas's class by recalling the Dreyfus affair. This would have been a hugely provocative gesture in 1924, and an exciting example of philosophy to a young Jewish intellectual recently arrived in France. Captain Alfred Dreyfus, an artillery officer from Alsace, in his day had been the highest ranking Jew in the French army. Falsely accused of treason and sentenced to life imprisonment on Devil's Island in 1894, he endured a long-drawn-out appeal and eventual exoneration. Indeed, although Dreyfus had returned to the army and had fought in the First World War, the French army itself did not formally acknowledge Dreyfus's innocence until 1995! The Affair, as it was known, was one of the most serious scandals of the French Third Republic and shook French social hierarchies definitively. Its repercussions led among other things to a 1905 French law separating Church and State, the more rapid emergence of a new intelligentsia in France and a radicalization of French nationalism that would carry on into the collaborationist Vichy regime during the Second World War. By the same token, however, it also contributed to the creation of the World Zionist Organization in 1897 by the young reporter Theodor Herzl, who had covered the affair and reached the conclusion that Jews could never receive proper justice in European society. So Pradines's illustration would have brought home to Levinas, in a way that appealed to personal experience as well as general intellect, how ethics could be both fundamental and immediately relevant.

The most decisive and lasting influence on Levinas from his student years, however, was undoubtedly his 1925 encounter with the critic and journalist Maurice Blanchot. This was, on the face of it, an unlikely pairing, given that at the time Blanchot affected monarchist political leanings and indeed was to write for right-wing nationalist publications which endorsed a politics of force right up to the defeat of France in June 1940. But as early as 1927, Blanchot introduced Levinas to the French literature of Proust and Valéry, while Levinas for his part explained to Blanchot the phenomenology of Husserl and, later, Heidegger. After the defeat of France, during which Blanchot helped to save Levinas's wife and daughter from the Nazis, Blanchot's subtle and profound writings undertook to elaborate a deep and fundamental abandonment of the aesthetics connected to the disastrous dream of a new French nationalism. This huge transformation was to parallel in certain key respects Levinas's own critique of Western philosophy from the late thirties on. In the post-war period, then, the two thinkers continued to build a deep philosophical dialogue in their respective works that lasted right up to Levinas's death. In the late sixties and beyond, for example, Blanchot's writing develops post-Holocaust concerns and resonances that are impregnated with key Levinasian notions like responsibility and passivity. For his part, nine years before his death, Levinas was to describe their friendship as being no less than a 'moral elevation' (IRB 29).

FREIBURG

One of Levinas's most exciting intellectual moments at Strasbourg came when he read for the first time the *Logical Investigations* (1900–01) by Edmund Husserl. Considered one of the founding texts of phenomenology, the work seeks to present philosophy as the science of consciousness rather than of empirical things. In other words, phenomenology will not look at how we collect data and then arrive at a theory, but rather at the essential nature of perceptual experience itself. Fired by this new philosophy for a new age, Levinas promptly went to Freiburg to study under Husserl himself in 1928–29, before writing his thesis on Husserl's theory of intuition, which he defended on 4 April 1930 and published immediately afterwards. At the same time, he co-translated Husserl's *Cartesian Meditations* into French, which was published in 1931, thus they appeared in France twenty years before they saw the light of day in Germany. With these publications, Levinas effectively introduced phenomenology into France at the ripe age of 26.

Yet this intellectual development in itself immediately became part of a dynamic duality. In Levinas's notable phrase: 'I went to see Husserl and I found Heidegger' (IRB 32). Martin Heidegger had been proposed by Husserl himself as his successor at Freiburg, and indeed inherited the latter's chair in 1928. His *Being and Time*, published the previous year, presented a dramatic new articulation of modern humanity's loss of authentic Being, with the philosophically strange notions of authenticity, anxiety, being-in-the-world and destiny assuming a defining status. While championing Husserl's work, then, it is ironic that Levinas also parti-cipated in its immediate demise in more ways than one. Not only did Levinas give the final exposé in the last tutorial of Husserl's final course prior to retirement, but his eventual thesis significantly opened up criticisms of Husserl from a distinctly Heideggerian 'historical' perspective, which he described himself as 'post-Husserlian' (TIHP 130). Prior to this, Levinas had attended classes taken by Heidegger, who also supported Levinas's application to attend a conference at Davos, held in March 1929. Levinas's earliest articles offered excited endorsement of Heideggerian being, and the conference itself was to confirm the almost revolutionary impact of Heidegger's thought on a young generation of thinkers.

PHENOMENOLOGY

Twentieth-century field of philosophical speculation closely associated with Husserl. Developing out of Kant's distinction between consciousness and content, and Hegel's dialectical view of how self-consciousness forms fully, phenomenology elaborates a complex investigation of the relationship between the act of consciousness itself and the objects or phenomena towards which consciousness is directed.

EDMUND HUSSERL (1859–1938)

German-language mathematician and founder of phenomenology, who wrote the massive *Logical Investigations* first published in 1900–01. He brings the Kantian division between mental processes and things into the modern age by investigating how the content of thought exists intrinsically within the mental act. His phenomenology therefore advances a reflective study of the very essence of consciousness.

MARTIN HEIDEGGER (1889–1976)

German existentialist educated at Freiburg under Husserl, whose university chair he inherited. Regarded as one of the most radical philosophers of the twentieth century, but tainted by his association with Nazism. His dense and ambitious *Being and Time* (1927) argues that philosophy needs to return to the essential question of being, and focuses on *Dasein* or the temporal being for whom existence itself is a question. Heidegger's later work, after the war, included a fatalist and critical view of the modern world, with its democratic and technologically driven modes of being.

DAVOS

The Swiss ski resort of Davos is today best known perhaps as the location for the annual gathering of the World Economic Forum. In 1928, however, it was the significantly 'neutral' site for a more intellectual *rapprochement* between France and Germany, in the aftermath of the First World War. This first Davos conference featured the presence of such representative and fundamentally modern figures as the German theoretical physicist Albert Einstein, the Swiss psychologist Jean Piaget and the French sociologists Lucien Lévy-Bruhl and Marcel Mauss. But in the following year of 1929, at the conference attended by Levinas, these humanitarian efforts were dramatically tested by the starkly competing views of Kant presented by the philosopher Ernst Cassirer, on the one hand, and by Heidegger on the other hand. Levinas later sought to convey the full historical weight of this event with an ambiguous description: '[a]t the time, it probably represented the end of a certain humanism, but perhaps today a fundamental antinomy and profound antiquity, of our civilization and of humanity' (IRB 34).

Cassirer was a former student of Hermann Cohen, the first Jew to hold a professorship at a German university. By 1929 Cassirer himself had become the first Jewish rector of a German university, until he was forced to resign his position at Hamburg in 1933, with the rise to power of the Nazis. Cassirer referred to Heidegger's *Being and Time* while essentially reiterating his own work on *The Philosophy of Symbolic Forms* to argue for the existence of objectively valid, necessary and eternal truths. By contrast, Heidegger (taking Cohen as his target as much as Kant) presented the existential situation of *Dasein*, or temporal being for whom existence is a question, in a way that looked to make science derivative to the understanding of being. To the impressionable students, Cassirer represented the past, and Heidegger the exciting future. In Levinas's own recollection, this judgement was delivered playfully but cruelly in the form of a review performed by the students and attended by Heidegger and Cassirer, in which the latter, played by Levinas himself, was made to reply weakly to Heidegger's repeated attacks: 'I'm a pacifist' (IRB 187).

Levinas's recollections of the Davos conference obviously go well beyond the details of an academic debate and the pranks of callow youth. He retrospectively locates in this one moment the demise of an entire thinking inspired by Kant and the Enlightenment (IRB 187), and an advance warning of the rise of National Socialism with which Heidegger was to be formally associated in the early thirties (IRB 35). While this may sound excessive, it is clear that, beyond the actual debate itself, Levinas takes Cassirer to be symbolically representative here of Husserl, philosophies of intellectual freedom and even perhaps all Jewish intellectuals, and that Heidegger's intellectual position therefore somehow prefigures the imminent rise of irrationalist evil and anti-Semitism. Levinas undoubtedly has in mind here a number of facts: how Heidegger had dedicated *Being and Time* to Husserl on its publication, and removed this dedication when it was reprinted in 1941; how in April 1933 Husserl was temporarily banned by racial laws from using the university library at Freiburg, while Heidegger in the same month became rector of that same university; and how Heidegger wrote to Husserl on 29 April, joined the Nazi party on 3 May and on 27 May made nationalistic exhortations in his traditional rectorship address. For Levinas, this goes beyond hypocrisy and grubby ambition. War, anti-Semitism and the ominous rise of an intolerant and seductive philosophy of force become combined in Levinas's recollection of the Davos conference.

IMMANUEL KANT (1724–1804)

German Enlightenment philosopher who wrote *Critique of Pure Reason* (1781), *Critique of Practical Reason* (1788) and *Critique of Judgement* (1790). His massively influential work looks to reconcile idealism and materialism. Kant believes that knowledge is not just the accumulation of encounters with the material world, but instead depends on the conceptual process of our own understanding, which itself is not derived from experience.

HERMANN COHEN (1842–1918)

Described as one of the most important Jewish philosophers of the nineteenth century, and a founder of the Marburg School of *neo-Kantianism*, which generally emphasized scientific readings of Kant's ideas, with a stress on concepts rather than intuition. Politically, some of his ideas became associated with socialism. Author of *Kant's Foundations of Ethics* (1877) and *Religion of Reason out of the Sources of Judaism* (1919).

ERNST CASSIRER (1874–1945)

German-language philosopher, originally trained by the Marburg School, is considered a major intellectual historian as well as *neo-Kantian* philosopher. His *Philosophy of Symbolic Forms* (1923–29), which looks to reconcile scientific and non-scientific modes of thought, is regarded as a classic text in the philosophy of culture. Went into exile in 1933 and eventually emigrated to the United States, where he taught at Yale and Columbia. His final work, *The Myth of the State* (1946), written in English and published posthumously, traces the irrationalism of Fascism back to philosophical roots.

FALLINGBOSTEL

Levinas became a French citizen in 1931 and did his military service the following year. He remained proud of both facts. In 1934 he accepted a job as administrator in the Alliance Israélite Universelle, an organization seeking to secure the emancipation of Jews in the non-European countries of the Mediterranean basin where they enjoyed no citizenship rights. The Alliance's modernizing work had an important educational dimension, and Levinas was to become director of its teacher-training programme, the Paris-based École Normale Israélite Orientale (ENIO), after the war. This essentially bureaucratic work gave Levinas the basic security and means to get married (in 1932) and to begin a family (a daughter was born in 1935). But nonetheless he tried to continue with philosophy, even though he soon had to digest the implications of Heidegger's endorsement of Nazism, which he reflected in a 1934 article on the philosophy of Hitlerism (produced presciently a year before Hitler actually became Führer) as well as in a short work of anguished revolt entitled *On Escape*, which he later described as written 'on the eve of great massacres' (OE 1). By now political events in Europe were deteriorating rapidly. When Heidegger resigned his rectorship on 23 April 1934, the Gestapo had already been formed, books by Jews had been burned, the Nazis had been declared the only party in Germany and Germany itself had left the League of Nations. French domestic politics were also becoming violently polarized, with the collapse of the Popular Front government, a growing influx of refugees from Eastern Europe and a concomitant anti-Semitic backlash. At the outbreak of war in 1939, Levinas was mobilized, only to be quickly taken prisoner at Rennes, in a rout of the French 10th Army, on 16 June 1940. He was deported to Stalag XIB, and from there to a forest labour camp at Fallingbostel, outside Hannover. Spared the fate of many Jews by virtue of being in French uniform, Levinas was treated as a regular prisoner of war. He survived the next four years in conditions of tough work, isolation, cold and hunger. Levinas would later recount how only a local dog treated the prisoners as humans, and seemed to be the last Kantian in Germany. Key sections of Levinas's immediate post-war texts, notably *Existence and Existents*, were begun or formed here. It was only after repatriation, at the end of the war, that he learned of the murder of almost his entire family in the Nazi Final Solution, with the exception of his wife and daughter, whom Blanchot had first hidden in Paris and then placed safely in a St Vincent de Paul monastery near Orléans. Lithuanian Jewry suffered some of the worst atrocities of the Shoah. Ninety-one per cent of the Jewish population there was killed by the Nazis, and in his home town of Kaunas, Lithuanian nationalists sided with the invading German forces and assisted in the murder of 30,000 Jews over a four-month period. The dedication of Levinas's 1974 *Otherwise than Being* later magnificently bore witness to the massive loss inflicted on all confessions and nations by a fundamental hatred of the other. And it was recognition of the other that became the guiding principle of Levinas's post-war philosophy.

SHOAH

The destruction and murder of European Jewry by the Nazis (led by Adolf Hitler) and their accomplices between 1933 and 1945. The term is preferred by some Jewish writers to that of the Holocaust, because of the latter's theological connotations. The Final Solution was a term used to refer to the development of mass extermination programmes, inflicted predominantly on Jews by the Nazis, at the height of the Second World War.

PARIS

Returning to his family in Paris after the war, Levinas became director of the ENIO in 1946 and remained in that position right up until the sixties. Only then, after defending his doctoral thesis, did he enter university teaching for the first time, even though publication of the important transitional works *Existence and Existents*, *Time and the Other* and *Discovering Existence with Husserl and Heidegger* meant that Levinas was already known within specialist circles for his development of an ethical critique of ontology. In contrast to the thirties, this period was one of stability for Levinas. A son was born at the end of the forties. The Levinas family lived above the school, and observed pedagogical and religious as well as domestic rhythms. Paris naturally provided a stimulating intellectual environment for Levinas, even if he remained relatively unknown publicly as a philosopher, and he was not in sympathy with the driving anti-humanism of the post-war French thought most in vogue. He lectured at the newly formed Collège Philosophique, attended Kojève's trend-setting seminars on Hegel at the École Pratique des Hautes Études, and participated in the French Philosophical Society. But just as important for Levinas's post-war intellectual development during this time was a much more personal form of engagement, involving a long and intense study of the Talmud, that massive compilation of rabbinic discussions about Jewish law and ethics. One outlet for this new practice was Levinas's introduction to the ENIO's otherwise modernist curriculum of a Talmudic class which he himself conducted on Saturday mornings after the Sabbath service. Another was an annual Talmudic reading which Levinas gave to the Colloquium of French-speaking Jewish Intellectuals from 1959 on. Both undertakings clearly indicate a search for philosophical renewal by Levinas through a particular return to traditional sources, notwithstanding his careful insistence that his philosophical and 'Judaic' activities were separate.

A formative influence on Levinas during the most intense period of such study was the enigmatic itinerant Talmudic teacher Chouchani. This reputedly difficult person, who stayed with the Levinas family for two or three years and then abruptly left, possessed not only an extraordinary knowledge of Scriptures but an impressive analytic ability that, in Levinas's words, made 'an always restless dialectic rebound sovereignly' (IRB 75). It was a skill that Chouchani implacably demonstrated in classes sometimes lasting six hours and ending at two in the morning. The effect of his teaching is acknowledged in the introduction to Levinas's first published set of Talmudic readings, where Levinas endorses a mode of reading that is significantly described as existing 'after the Liberation', one which is engaged in a new search for 'problems and truths' (NTR 9) that cannot rely on previous approaches. This deeply textual re-turn was to be developed by Levinas in readings published over the course of the following twenty years. It is self-consciously a different form of tenacious commitment that parallels and sometimes even leads his precise philosophical research after the war. In their different registers, both sets of writings also engage with the more general French scene of political and intellectual reconstruction, from the fifties right through to the seventies.

Levinas's publication in 1961 of his major thesis, *Totality and Infinity*, belatedly announced his arrival as a considerable figure of philosophy. Subsequently, his late career as a university teacher began at Poitiers in the same year, before he moved in 1967 to the new campus at Nanterre. His arrival almost coincided, however, with the eruption of student demonstrations, set off initially by educational reforms that same year, but symbolizing the overdue breakdown of a post-war political consensus in France. As one of the new universities catering for the boom in student numbers and focusing on newer subjects with a critical edge, principally in the social sciences, Nanterre was a natural breeding-ground for student protest, and the campus was occupied in March 1968. The philosopher Paul Ricœur, who had recruited Levinas to the faculty, sought to mediate, but was badly shaken by his experience of violence on the part of both agitators and police, and eventually departed for the University of Chicago. Blanchot, on the other hand, whose politics had by now moved greatly to the left, demonstrated in favour of unrest in the main courtyard of the Sorbonne. In general, the social agitation of this time, known thereafter as May '68, was actually rather short-lived, not least as the aims of students were in reality rather different from those of workers. But idealistically, the events became enshrined as the defining moment when a still dominant conservative morality in France was openly challenged in the name of human rights, sexual liberation and equality. Levinas was largely unsympathetic to such a revolution in attitudes, not only for social and cultural reasons but also out of respect for learning and the ideals of a French Republic for which he felt strong intellectual and emotional loyalties. When he could, he gave his classes, confining himself in his writings of the period to obliquely dismissive references to structuralism and anti-humanist thinking. When the opportunity arose in 1973, Levinas moved from the radicalizing

Nanterre to the more conservative Sorbonne, where he gave classes on phenomenology up to his retirement in 1976.

ALEXANDRE KOJÈVE (1902–68)

Political philosopher born in Russia. From 1933 to 1939 gave a series of lectures on Hegel which influenced succeeding generations of French thinkers, critics and analysts. Through Leo Strauss, his thesis on 'the End of History' was also taken up by certain influential political theorists in the United States.

GEORG WILHELM FRIEDRICH (GWF) HEGEL (1770–1831)

German philosopher who wrote *Phenomenology of Spirit* (1807), *Lectures on Aesthetics* (1820) and the *Philosophy of Right* (1826). He established *dialectics* as a dominant form of modern philosophical inquiry. Dialectics involves working through two apparent contradictions in order to achieve a third greater knowledge. Hegel uses dialectics to enquire into the conditions of thought.

PAUL RICŒUR (1913–2005)

Major French, Protestant philosopher, influenced by phenomenology and hermeneutics. Among his many major works are *The Conflict of Interpretations* (1969), the three-volume *Time and Narrative* (1983–85), *Oneself as Another* (1990) and *Memory, History, Forgetting* (2000).

ISRAEL

In the seventies, a flurry of publications, including most importantly his radical and challenging *Otherwise than Being* in 1974, confirmed Levinas as a major figure of phenomenology. In spite of this, he was more often an observer than a commentator in many of the French and even European socio-cultural debates of the day. This was partly consistent with his ethical philosophy, which stressed that politics must come 'after'. But at the same time, developing social trends meant that Levinas's works by now were not only generating overdue praise, but also garnering fundamental criticisms. Two recurring negative views, for example, which began to be voiced during this time were that the feminine alterity, or ideal woman, projected in Levinas's writings supported an ethical agency that was implicitly masculine, and that his work explicitly valorized a uniquely Eurocentric and Judaeo-Christian set of references. It is certainly true that Levinas is silent, at least directly, on such contemporary issues as the struggle to legalize abortion in France, which came about in 1974–75, or the many obvious ethical issues relating to growing communities of North African origin in France's cities. In fact, the politics of ethics for Levinas are henceforth located far less in Europe's social directions than in the significance and repercussions of the 1967 Six-Day War which Israel conducted with the Arab states of Egypt, Jordan, Iraq and Syria. Some of Levinas's radical philosophical postulations of proximity and obsession, or substitution and justice, also recur, then, in his evocations of a profoundly messianic and inherently ethical Israel. A typical example of Levinas's vision is an article published in April 1968, entitled 'Space is not One-dimensional'. Defending the State of Israel's position after the recent Six-Day War, Levinas suggests to France that it should rediscover its own religious sources, such that the nation's Republican values of Liberty, Equality and Fraternity would be joined by a fourth term, Religion. Such an institutionalization of ethics might not have succeeded brilliantly in a France that was actually on the point of erupting into May '68. But the vision of Israel (rather than France) that actually drives the suggestion depends once again on a dramatic dualism. Levinas's Israel here is an absolute ethical entity rather more than it is a political reality. What he envisages is really a state beyond a state, and an ethical existence beyond essence. His evocations of Israel throughout the seventies and eighties therefore expressed aspirations and ideals rather than *realpolitik*.

Acknowledging the ethical nature of this social vision, but also registering dissension from it, including perhaps his own, Jacques Derrida stressed how Levinas himself always encouraged us 'to read what we thought we had already read under his signature' (AEL 9). Derrida made this observation in a funeral oration at Pantin cemetery, two days after Levinas's death on 25 December 1995. While contemporary political events will no doubt continue to disappoint a Levinasian vision, it is clear already that the works of Levinas themselves will continue to provide the most complete example of phenomenology's development over the course of the twentieth century, an inspirational and challenging model of thinking wholly otherwise, and a rich textual basis for the endless practice of critical rereading.

JACQUES DERRIDA (1930–2004)

Algerian-born French philosopher known as the founder of *deconstruction*, a form of analysis that was especially influential in the 1970s. Based on the idea that Western thinking advanced one idea by excluding or subjugating another, deconstruction elaborated complex readings that sought in themselves to resist establishing in this way a new hierarchy of values. The term *différance*, coined by Derrida, was used to suggest this aim by indicating simultaneous difference and deferral, in part through its spelling which can only be appreciated in a written or textual form rather than in an oral and supposedly immediate manner.

2

PHENOMENOLOGY

The thirties (extending through the war into the forties) was a period of intense and rapid philosophical development for Levinas. He absorbed the revolutionary implications of phenomenology in the presence of its masters Husserl and Heidegger, and then effectively introduced this philosophy into France. In his own first publications, he explored the intoxicating freedom of these theories, and then had to revise his enthusiasm upon discovering Heidegger's endorsement of Nazism. As a result, he then began more patiently and painfully to construct the intricate ideas and approaches that were to underpin his mature ethics. So this chapter traces Levinas's initial indebtedness and subsequent questioning of phenomenology, it reads in detail some of the key explorations of experience, temporality and the emerging Other which Levinas elaborated during this period, and it points up the important connections to the later, major, works.

FROM HUSSERL TO HEIDEGGER

Levinas's writings begin in intellectual freedom and a pure phenomenological ambition. Even before he produces his own first philosophical attempts, Levinas reflects this exuberant state of being in his very first article, the confident and proselytizing 'On *Ideen*, by E. Husserl', published in 1929 while he was still studying in Freiburg under Husserl. It rejoices in announcing this 'new science', with its 'great depth and originality'. It is 'a totally new way' (UH 25–26) of thinking, which obliges us to change our attitudes radically and put aside our scepticism (UH 35). In fact, with the benefit of hindsight, it is very noticeable how scepticism and affirmations about God, cornerstones of Levinas's mature work, are here explicitly excluded from discussion (UH 34, 41). Levinas's article clearly and dutifully explains core Husserlian concepts and even borrows Husserl's own examples. But in doing this, he is equally differentiating himself from his 'French' training, represented here and later by Bergson, and so often pointedly approves of Husserl's observations at the expense of Bergson's views on, say, consciousness or time. In fact, Levinas does not stop transferring loyalties at this point, for he also raises, in a final section on 'Intersubjective reduction', a number of problems that he says still have to be pondered. It is significant that here he mentions Husserl's unpublished writings, for Heidegger was already working with this material (UH 56).

A complementary piece, 'Freiburg, Husserl, and Phenomenology', published two years later, is altogether more journalistic, and displays even more clearly a certain naivety in this newfound intellectual freedom. Retrospectively, we can see how the account naively contains hints of the darker climate that is to come. Levinas speaks of an 'inebriation in work ... combined with joyful enthusiasm. For the young Germans I met at Freiburg, the new philosophy is more than a new theory; it is a new ideal of life, a new page in history, almost a new religion' (UH 63). Here, too, Heidegger makes a late entrance as Husserl's 'most original disciple', in a narrative that cheerfully tells us that only a privileged few are able to attend his lectures, and that his 'name is now Germany's glory' (UH 64).

This fascination with Heidegger, which was abruptly brought to an end by the revelation of Heidegger's involvement with the Nazi party, can also be seen in what remains of an abandoned book on Heidegger. This book would have explained Heidegger's *Being and Time* and effectively argued for his replacement of Husserl as the key phenomenologist. Traces of this abandoned project can be glimpsed in a 1932 article 'Martin Heidegger and Ontology'. Usefully, a significantly amended version of this eventually appeared in the 1949 book *Discovering Existence with Husserl and Heidegger*. As a result, we can see how Levinas's views changed. The foreword to the book specifies that the inclusion of the article was in no way intended as a post-war apology for 'a philosophy that does not always guarantee wisdom' (DEHH 5). Alerted to this tension, we notice how there are subtle but decisive differences between the two versions. At certain points, Heidegger quite simply has his crown removed, most obviously when the original article's opening two paragraphs, beginning: '[t]he prestige of Martin Heidegger and the influence of his thought on German philosophy marks both a new phase and one of the high points of the phenomenological movement' (MHO 11), are just cut.

This turn of events means that Levinas's subsequent works of the period are bound up with the need for involved revision. So his 1940 article on 'The Work of Edmund Husserl', with which *Discovering Existence* significantly, i.e. non-chronologically, opens, strongly rehabilitates Husserl's pre-eminence over Heidegger. In the immediate context of war and persecution, it is significant that it does so above all in terms of freedom. We are therefore told that 'Husserl's phenomenology is, in the final analysis, a philosophy of freedom', whereas in Heidegger, '[t]he subject is neither free nor absolute' but on the contrary is 'dominated and overwhelmed' (DEH 84). In Husserl, we are told, meaning is not determined by history, whereas Heidegger's approach 'undermines clarity and constitution' (DEH 87), and gives 'an interpretation of existence in its least intellectual forms' (DEH 87). The philosopher who so recently excited Levinas is now aligned philosophically with the forces of irrationalism and even totalitarianism.

ONTOLOGY

From the Greek word for being, ontology means the study of being or existence and the ways in which we might categorize entities, and so talk objectively about essence and existence. The process can be traced back to Aristotle. Heidegger's *Being and Time* describes philosophy as ontology, but claims to pursue the question of being in a concrete rather than a general manner.

HENRI BERGSON (1859–1941)

French philosopher. Rejecting mechanistic explanations of the natural world, emphasized the subjective experience of time as the ground for human freedom in his 1889 *Essay on the Immediate Data of Consciousness* and the 1896 *Matter and Memory*. His 1907 *Creative Evolution* postulated that thought, creativity, motion and evolution are all products of a single creative impulse or *élan vital*.

SCEPTICISM

The philosophical term scepticism has its roots in Ancient Greek philosophy, and indicates a form of inquiry that does not believe we can ever reach certain knowledge.

THE THEORY OF INTUITION

Between producing his earliest pieces, Levinas had also published his philosophy thesis, *The Theory of Intuition in Husserl's Phenomenology*, in 1930. It dutifully follows Husserl's grounding of science in consciousness, intentionality, objectification and intuition. As the title suggests, this final area is central to Levinas's analysis. Here, however, Levinas does begin to cross-examine Husserl's conception of consciousness more robustly, and in a conclusion to the chapter on philosophical intuition, an independent Levinas who is recognizable by us begins to emerge for the first time, when he significantly states that the reduction to an *ego* 'can be only a first step towards phenomenology. We must also discover "others" [*les "autres"*] and the intersubjective world' (TIHP 150). At this stage, though, Levinas still exploits both Heidegger and Bergson in an attempt to fashion this independent position. He therefore notes both that the world is 'a field of activity or of *care* – to speak the language of Martin Heidegger' (TIHP 119), and that we can use Bergson to expose Husserl's intuitionism of 'the act of freedom' (TIHP 155). We still have a choice, in other words, between a Bergsonian view of subjectivity and the existential vision of destiny in Heidegger. For the young Levinas, the evidence that influences such a choice, where free activity is assumed and developed, is still primarily philosophical and intellectual. Crucially, such choices are about to become exposed as fragile and even illusory, and Levinas will be forced to undergo a painful and fundamental revision of philosophical reduction itself.

ON ESCAPE

'It is dominated by the presentiment and the memory of the Nazi horror' (DF 291). Levinas's summary of his own intellectual biography, starkly presented as a separate paragraph in the closing, self-reflexive article of *Difficult Freedom* entitled 'Signature', indicates the most brutal invasion and subsequent domination by politics of his intellectual formation. The political and the ethical collide for Levinas, as a phenomenologist and a Jew, when the beginnings of the Shoah in 1933 coincide disastrously with Heidegger's acceptance of the rectorship at Freiburg and his public association with the Nazi party. The shock administered to Levinas's understanding of freedom is quickly reflected in the writings of the period, which are in themselves remarkable for their ability to formulate so quickly and clearly the fundamental change that was happening to the intellectual and political climate. A key philosophical text for Levinas's future development, then, is the place where he first tries to reverse his involvement with Heidegger's ontology. This is *On Escape*, first published in 1935. As Levinas poignantly puts it himself, his text retrospectively becomes a 'witness to an intellectual situation of meaning's end' (OE 1). It effectively dismantles what Levinas had confidently erected philosophically up to this point. *Escape* now symptomatically replaces freedom. Levinas places this urgent and even obsessive need at the origin of the experience of being. Through eight numbered sections, the text pursues a seemingly impossible goal of existential escape, dramatizing the situation of Being as it both posits itself and looks to escape from itself. Levinas's attempts to understand and so move beyond this point are obviously driven in part here by the vague but intimidating presence of a political horror that throws definitions of being and the search for refuge into crisis (OE 53). The text is forced to concede that inherited philosophical equipment is useless to combat this situation. This obviously includes Bergson, for Levinas states that the need to escape should not be confused with a Bergsonian life force (*l'élan vital*) or creative evolution (*devenir créateur*) (OE 53). But it most obviously involves Heidegger. In a phrase that evokes both Heidegger's philosophy and the 'presentiment' of political crisis, Levinas writes damningly that '[e]very civilization that accepts being – with the tragic despair it contains and the crimes it justifies – merits the name "barbarian"' (OE 73). The 'originality' of this thought is nonetheless deferred for now by Levinas, for to follow through with its consequences at this stage would somehow risk 'overturning certain notions that to common sense and the wisdom of the nations seemed the most evident' (OE 73). The ambiguous phrase leaves open the clear suggestion, however, that those nations were foolish, and that madness is about to prevail.

Looking ahead, it is the thematics of *Existence and Existents* and the more redemptive *Time and the Other* which will retroactively try to plot the escape that is outlined here as necessary. Indeed, anticipating Levinas's much later work, we can even glimpse in *On Escape* the anticipatory knowledge of a radical ethics articulated within *Otherwise than Being*, some forty years later. So the escape from being that is being recorded here as anguish actually prefigures the most radical phenomenological attempts in Levinas to break out of finitude. This happens not least because philosophical language and scenarios have been obliged here to break out of inherited forms.

THE PHILOSOPHY OF HITLERISM

The coming barbarism that the closing passages of *On Escape* seem to sense is pinpointed in a remarkably clear-sighted way in the contemporary article 'Reflections on the Philosophy of Hitlerism'. This was published in the progressive Catholic journal *Esprit* in 1934, shortly after Hitler's accession to power. On the occasion of its first translation into English, in 1990, Levinas described the circumstances and convictions of the piece. He stressed that 'the source of the bloody barbarism of National Socialism' (RPH 63) was due not to a moment of madness or to an ideological aberration but to 'the essential possibility of *elemental Evil* into which we can be led by logic and against which Western philosophy had not sufficiently insured itself' (RPH 63).

This already reinforces the anguished apprehension of *On Escape*, but Levinas goes further. Whereas the original article itself does not mention Heidegger by name, this prefatory addition now asserts that this possibility of evil 'is inscribed within the ontology of a being concerned with being – a being, to use the Heideggerian expression, "dem es in seinem Sein um dieses Sein selbst geht"' (RPH 63). Indeed, he adds in a determined tone that such a possibility still threatens, and that we have to ask ourselves if liberalism is all we need to achieve dignity for the human subject.

In the actual piece, Levinas clearly introduces the anguished body of *On Escape* into a more historico-political framework. A 'primary' and primitive Hitlerism is actually 'philosophically interesting' to Levinas, since it throws into crisis 'the very principles of a civilization' and so challenges not just political definitions of freedom but also the ahistorical notion of freedom as spirit (RPH 64). Levinas therefore reviews the Western concept of freedom, concluding that only with a proper phenomenological awareness of our body, where our situation forms the foundation of our being, do we get beyond a body–mind dualism. What is crucial here is that such a dualism can endorse, when enacted in force, '[t]he mysterious urgings of the blood, the appeals of heredity and the past for which the body serves as an enigmatic vehicle' (RPH 69).

From this point Levinas directly links a drama of destiny with racialist essentializations, making open allusions to Nietzsche, as well as indirect ones to Heidegger. In so doing he noticeably turns racialist language back on itself: it is civilization that is 'invaded' by everything that is not 'authentic', as a society that has lost its true ideal of freedom accepts 'degenerate' forms of the ideal (RPH 70). Recalling his earlier *On Escape*, he claims that an acceptance of racial purity sees man 'himself refusing the power to escape from himself' through the contemplation of truth. As a result, truth itself becomes embroiled in an existential drama, universalism becomes converted into the idea of 'the expansion of a force' and those who accept this distortion now constitute 'a community of "masters"' (RPH 70). Levinas concludes this powerful denunciation by demonstrating how freedom itself is thus quite logically replaced by force in this 'philosophy'. Pointedly, he adds that this is precisely 'Nietzsche's will to power, which modern Germany is rediscovering and glorifying' (RPH 71). What this phrase really signifies more personally for Levinas is a denunciation of Heidegger, who in Levinas's still recent words had also been called 'Germany's glory' (UH 64). Levinas's prophetic warning proved to be horribly accurate. In his immediate post-war writings, therefore, he would attempt in certain key ways to re-build a non-mastering community. As we shall see, this would also involve a more explicit foregrounding of his Jewish heritage.

FRIEDRICH NIETZSCHE (1844–1900)

German philosopher who wrote provocative critiques of the Western philosophical tradition and of Christianity that sought to advocate a naturalistic morality and to recognize the basic impulse of a 'will to power'. The concept was appropriated by some Nazi apologists. Best-known works include *Daybreak* (1881), *Thus Spoke Zarathustra* (1883–85), *Beyond Good and Evil* (1886) and *The Anti-Christ* (1888).

EXISTENCE AND EXISTENTS

Levinas survived the Second World War and the Holocaust by virtue of being in French uniform. Most of his family were murdered, along with at least six million others, the majority Jews. The Stalag where Levinas survived the war and the Final Solution as a forced labourer, and wrote the core sections of *Existence and Existents*, is mentioned with chilling calm in the work's preface. Survival becomes much more than just a historical moment here, though. Philosophically, it generates a real move away from ontology and from seemingly inadequate concepts of Being, which are now associated with totalitarianism, massacre and horror. The exceptionally involved and dense account of minute experiences of survival in *Existence and Existents*, published almost immediately after the war in 1947, makes it tempting to read the text as a dark night of the soul. But this would overlook the positive and even revolutionary dimensions of the work, which begins to formulate a non-ontological experience of being, and brings us in the process through the unavoidable fatigue of being towards such hopeful terms as sociality, alterity, fecundity, hope and paternity.

The book's introduction clearly states a 'profound need' to leave the 'climate' (EE 20) of Heideggerian Being understood *as* anxiety, in order to investigate the anxiety *over* Being which is termed 'horror' (EE 20). The English translation of the book's title incidentally loses sight of this defining movement *from* existence *to* existents. In stark contrast to Heidegger's *Letter on Humanism*, produced initially for a French audience in the same year of 1947, Levinas's work is plotting a course precisely *away from* existence (Being) and *towards* the existent (being). We therefore move away from Heideggerian questions about Being or existential struggle and care, towards a new, denuded, sense of being as fatigue and effort. There is nothing heroic or authentic in these forms of being, nor do they lead to understanding or a relationship with being. They are just minimal conditions that radically challenge the idea of freedom inherent for Levinas in Western philosophical accounts from Plato through Marxism to Heidegger.

Such a freedom with respect to being breaks down dramatically in the following chapter, where Levinas introduces the elemental notion of the *there is*. This key description is not only found at the heart of the text but actually predetermines the work's entire vision. It was written by Levinas while he was in captivity and was published in 1946, prior to the book's whole appearance. Its importance and strangeness derive from the way in which it attempts to evoke the collapse of the entire philosophical or rational comprehension of horror. The haunting result is perhaps one of the most overwhelming evocations of the experience of pure being in twentieth-century writing. The *there is* is described as being in general, but not something that can be derived as a notion from any being, since distinctions between interiority and exteriority disappear before it. It is shown to be immediately there, in the night, as a silence, but it does not exist in a dialectical relationship with absence. It is what does not and cannot disappear when everything else, including the I, has disappeared. It is a nocturnal space, one that is not empty but rather is full only of the nothingness of everything (EE 58). It cannot be intelligibly understood: neither Bergsonian nothingness nor Heideggerian anxiety can conceptualize this 'fatality of irremissible being' (EE 61). The *there is* can only be experienced as a horror, from which we cannot even escape by dying, or sleeping or dreaming (Shakespeare is cited several times at this point, partly because philosophy texts are inadequate here, and partly in order to recall the horror experienced by Macbeth before the ghost of Banquo). Fundamentally, consciousness can provide no defence against the *there is*, which is experienced in a terrible and unavoidable wakefulness, or a permanent insomnia.

From this lowest point, where past formulations are useless and future ones cannot be seen, and as though re-building itself after complete trauma, the text then begins slowly to record the generation of tiny acts, out of which in turn a very fragile sense of freedom begins to develop. This minimal sense will never be free of the *there is* and it will be forever burdened with the weight and responsibility of its being. But out of this devastation will gradually emerge new foundations for being, which are significantly located in the alterity of the other and a transformed view of time. These are themselves founded on the notions of redemption and justice (EE 89). This new state of being can never recover the past: as we are told in a moment that is painful in its simplicity, 'pain cannot be redeemed' (EE 91). But it does, importantly, place a new emphasis on social relationships (EE 94), and gives rise to formulations that will later express the core of Levinas's future philosophy, such as neighbour, proximity, asymmetry and even substitution. From the extreme dereliction of the experience of *Existence and Existents*, then, there arises a radical hope. It is a hope that is expressed politically in the work's conclusion that it has been concerned with 'the meaning of the very fact that in Being there are beings' (EE 101). But it is given no less powerfully, if more personally, in the penultimate chapter's final thought that the subject now 'has the possibility of not inevitably returning to itself, the possibility of being fecund and ... having a son' (EE 96). These human possibilities are taken up and given their clearest and most programmatic expression yet in Levinas's next work, *Time and the Other*.

PLATO (C. 429–347 BCE)

Generally regarded as the founder of Western philosophical traditions. Produced a series of Dialogues that include *Phaedo*, *Republic*, *Theaetetus* and *Phaedrus*. The later ones present a concept of forms as being independent, real, invisible and unchanging. Perceiving these is what constitutes knowledge, whereas belief about the changing world is just opinion or *doxa*. The *Republic* compares order and justice as found in the State and in the soul, and gives a famous analogy of the cave (and shadows) that seeks to show that only those who can perceive the form of the good are fit to rule. The *Theaetetus* establishes a classical notion of knowledge as being true belief that is validated by reason.

TIME AND THE OTHER

Time and the Other is composed of four lectures delivered in 1946–47 at the Philosophical College in Paris. They were first published in this format in 1948 (in a collection dated 1947) before finally appearing as a book, together with a new preface, in 1979. Their lecture-based nature, and the fact that Levinas here often summarizes for a general audience the involved positions we have seen him work through, give this work a surprising directness and clarity. In addition, though, they also place strong emphasis on the future, above all encapsulated here in the way death is presented not as an end but as the opening onto infinity, and the closing evocations are of fecundity and paternity. *Time and the Other* is therefore a strategically important text for the way in which Levinas quickly resumes for himself a long philosophical formation and uses this summary to initiate a new phase of work which will gradually build towards the major post-war works *Totality and Infinity* and *Otherwise than Being*.

Time and the Other explores in neat succession the nature of being, solitude, materiality, entry into the world, suffering and mortality, encounter with the other, and the Other's significance. It gives the most summary disagreement so far with Heidegger, as well as with both Hegelian dialectics and the significance of Bergsonian duration. These confident and concrete distinctions establish the independent Levinasian voice of the post-war period. The work's core aim is to present time not as the 'achievement' of an isolated subject but as the 'relationship' of the subject with the Other (TO 39). This idea acts from the beginning as an open repudiation of the Heideggerian vision, where being is essentially solitude and where sociality is at best a 'being-with' (*Mitandersein*) rather than a face-to-face relationship. This solitude, however, is for Levinas exceeded by the 'mystery' of death, which is here understood positively as fundamental ungraspable alterity.

At this point Levinas introduces the *there is* which we encountered in *Existence and Existents*. In contrast to a Heideggerian anxiety and experience of nothingness, Levinas stresses how the *there is* confirms the *impossibility* of dying (TO 51). This condition in turn produces a fundamentally different conception of freedom, which is no longer based on 'virile power' (TO 54) or 'genial solitude' (TO 55). As Levinas realized in *On Escape*, identity is chained to itself (TO 55) or 'encumbered' (TO 56), and so cannot be explained by theories of classic idealism, constructive socialism or modern existentialism (TO 61). In a move that evokes images of birth and nurture even as Levinas here brings philosophy itself into a re-birth, he then contrasts an instrumental or antagonistic view of being in the world with the primary relationships of nourishment and enjoyment which he had evoked already in *Existence and Existents*, and which are also strategically recalled in later works. But to these he also positively adds the significance of suffering and death. For 'the absence of all refuge' in suffering and death (TO 69) means that our attitude to life is the opposite of the one suggested by a Heideggerian *being towards Death*. For Levinas, death, like freedom, will also remain fundamentally 'ungraspable' and beyond 'virility' (TO 72), and signifies 'the impossibility of having a project' (TO 74).

But this is entirely positive, for it moves us away from a relationship with the other that is based via death on antagonism or on communion. At no time do I assume the other, or project the other as a part of my freedom. Instead, the other in Levinas retains its alterity. Describing this as a non-reciprocity, Levinas personifies this relationship as the mystery of the feminine. It is a key evocation, which was also used to conclude *Existence and Existents*, and it is one that can generate its own problems, as we shall repeatedly see in reading some of his later works. For Levinas, though, the *feminine* is here meant to indicate less a sexual difference than a location and a mode of being that remain ungraspable, unmasterable and exceptional. Perhaps most significantly for him, this feminine is also an alterity through which the child, as *future* alterity, comes into being. As we recall, this was also the closing image of hope used by *Existence and Existents*.

Time and the Other serves for Levinas to mark the end of a certain metaphysics, but it also signals the hopeful embodiment of a different mode of being in a post-war climate. It acts, moreover, as an important connecting link in Levinas's writing. It retains from his early phenomenology the fundamentally moral nature of singularity, and brings this now resolutely into a vision of the future that escapes the finite concepts of freedom, forceful inquiry and mastery. Henceforth, the intellectual tendency towards totality will be resisted by the ethical recognition of infinity. It is this fundamental re-founding of phenomenology that Levinas's first major work of philosophy (first in being the founding of ethics as first philosophy) will now work to confirm.

SUMMARY

Phenomenology provided Levinas with his philosophical formation. His early writings reflect both the influence and the shock of Heidegger's association with Nazism. Thereafter a number of key ideas and terms emerge which are at the core of the mature work. Key areas of this period of Levinas's writing are:

- The initial reception of Husserl and Heidegger.
- The shift in the works written after 1933, including *On Escape*.
- The early article on the philosophy of Hitlerism.
- The immediate post-war books *Existence and Existents* and *Time and the Other*.

3

TOTALITY AND INFINITY

Totality and Infinity (1961), subtitled *An Essay on Exteriority*, is the first of Levinas's two most famous and sustained texts. Placing the terms of the title initially in opposition to one another, Levinas advances an explicit critique of the whole of Western philosophy based on ontology, which he sees as having an inherent tendency to generate totalizing concepts of being. This approach is insistently linked by Levinas to the early and late philosophy of Martin Heidegger. In a set of sweeping and reiterating passages, sustained by key arresting images, Levinas repeatedly rejects the synthesizing of phenomena in favour of a way of thinking that supposedly remains open to the other.

Levinas's fundamentally ethical vision is above all dramatically embodied by him in his presentation of the *face* of the other. This is one of Levinas's most crucial formulations. He presents the face not simply as a physical detail, but as a moment of infinity that goes beyond any *idea* which I can produce of the other. The very existence of this face challenges all our philosophical attempts to systematize and therefore to reduce the other. So for Levinas, the assessment and indeed the goal of human existence are always situated in the unavoidable light of infinity. The face issues us with an absolute ethical challenge, and our relation with the *other* which the face stands for is one that begins, in Levinas's ethics, even before self-consciousness emerges. This relation is therefore based not on ontology, but on an original responsibility for the other, which is unavoidably there for me from the beginning. This makes ethics, in Levinas's view, not just a secondary area of philosophy but, on the contrary, 'first philosophy' itself. This chapter reviews the general vision of *Totality and Infinity*, details its major terms and references, focuses on the crucially embodied nature of the absolute ethics that Levinas advances, and looks at some of the difficulties and even contradictions that exist at the heart of the work.

MORALITY OR POLITICS

Levinas prefaces *Totality and Infinity* with a provocative and somewhat apocalyptic contrast between morality and war. Beginning with an almost sarcastic speculation about whether or not morality merely makes us gullible, in contrast to war which gives us the raw truth of reality, Levinas immediately starts to associate the second of these with an 'ontological event' and the 'concept of totality, which dominates Western philosophy' (TI 21). In an early case of what is going to become a familiar approach as the book advances, Levinas abruptly introduces terms which gain their meaning more by evocation and opposition than by definition and defence. So we are told here that 'war does not manifest exteriority and the other as other' (TI 21), which seems to mean, then, that 'exteriority' is what we get when totality and ontology are broken open, the other is recognized and ontology is resisted morally.

These unsubstantiated claims are put forward in an almost prophetic or messianic way, rather than as stages in a logical argument. But Levinas embraces such an approach, as the way to break free from the process of offering philosophical evidence, and therefore to get back to an original relation with being that for him exists before and beyond totality and history. The danger is that such an approach, relying on terms like transcendence, infinity and revelation, could be dismissed as a purely spiritual rather than rational vision. Again, Levinas recognizes this possibility, but turns the tables by suggesting that the systems of totalization given by Western philosophy and history have merely tried and failed to contain the idea of infinity. Levinas then pointedly locates the idea of infinity inside the canon of Western philosophy itself. He cites, as he is fond of doing, Descartes's analysis of the idea of the infinite in his Third Meditation, he recalls

Plato's ruminations on the Good, he points to Aristotle's *outside* and he similarly raises the conclusions of Kant's practical philosophy, in order to argue that philosophy recognizes an ascendance beyond being. At the same time, Levinas presents this idea of infinity as being what goes beyond the limits of thought, such that it is actually the condition for *every* objective truth. He calls this infinity 'more objective than objectivity' (TI 26), and actually presents it as being the mind that exists before we start to produce ontological reduction, that is, 'the mind before it lends itself to the distinction between what it discovers by itself and what it receives from opinion' (TI 25).

The idea of infinity as primary also means that subjectivity is primarily moral. Since infinity in Levinas's view is perceived by us as a *revelation* of the Other, and more specifically is located in the face of the other, consciousness for Levinas is not first and foremost the practice of reducing and representing existence for ourselves, but is initially a *moral* event that recognizes and welcomes the already established and inexhaustible other.

With this emphasis, Levinas therefore also looks to establish the limits of phenomenology from within phenomenology itself. He is proposing a phenomenology that sees beyond phenomenology. This intention accounts for Levinas's very particular use of the term *ethics*, along with the repeated claim that ethics is an 'optics' (TI 23, 29, 78). *Totality and Infinity* will seek to fulfil and in fact surpass phenomenology by adhering to a metaphysical transcendence that reaches out towards the absolutely other.

ETHICS

From the Greek word for character. Study of those concepts involved in practical reasoning such as good, right, obligation or freedom. Traditionally viewed as one dependent branch of philosophy, after ontology and aesthetics.

ARISTOTLE (384–322 BCE)

Key philosopher of the beginning of a Western tradition. What remains of his work can be grouped under the categories of logic, physics, natural history, ethics and metaphysics. A traditional contrast with Plato presents Aristotle as being intensely interested in the details of the real world. His ethics is therefore regarded as appreciative of the complexities of human motivations. In the twentieth century, Aristotle became re-evaluated in part for his relevance to political theory.

RENÉ DESCARTES (1596–1650)

French mathematician regarded as the founder of modern philosophy. His best-known work is the 1641 *Meditations on First Philosophy* which includes objections by Descartes's contemporaries together with Descartes's replies to the objections. His theory of knowledge famously starts with the search for an undoubtable starting-point on which to build all the rest, leading to the belief that 'I think therefore I am'. This priority leads to what is known as Cartesian dualism, or separation of the mind and body into two distinct but interacting substances. His recourse to a supreme being to explain their interrelationship led to problems.

OTHER

A key term in Levinas's writing, indicating the ethical rather than just the real object of the self's ethical being. Variously written as Other or other, to denote the French terms *autre*, *Autre* and *Autrui*.

THE SAME AND THE OTHER

Totality and Infinity's first section proper throws down a challenge to 'the egoist spontaneity of the same' (TI 43) at the heart of ontology, which Levinas regards as being dedicated to self-perpetuation at the expense of the other. As ever, he associates this reduction of alterity with Heidegger, and here specifically with the latter's evocations of dwelling or *sojourning*, or being 'at home with oneself' (TI 37). Levinas views these metaphors as promoting a powerful form of being, which is at home in the world above all because it actually possesses it. These operations of the 'same' therefore have the effect of suspending or nullifying alterity. As a result, no true metaphysical relation can be entertained by this *I* and its powers, because alterity is merely formal in this set-up; whereas Levinas argues that the metaphysical other is not at all formal, or ever 'at home', in its fundamental and non-reducible alterity.

At this point Levinas produces a typical flurry of descriptions and analogies, partly to show how an exemplary ethical relation between same and other, in which the other remains transcendent, actually involves the language we use. So we are told that the metaphysical other (*autre*) is also both the absolutely other (*l'absolument Autre*) and the Other (*Autrui*). In addition, this other or Other is also personified as 'the Stranger who disturbs the being at home with oneself', or 'the free one' who is not wholly 'in my site' (TI 39). Later this same figure, by association, somehow becomes 'the infinite, the transcendent' (TI 49). The driving point is that Levinas does not want to present the relationship between the same and the other as adding up to a totality, and so the other must not be categorized. This can produce basic difficulties for Levinas's own language and exposition, of course, and the way in which he is led to appeal to a wide range of intellectual and spiritual categories, while simultaneously seeking to resist the effects of categorization, can be just confusing on occasions.

Some of this confusion lifts, though, when Levinas starts to locate the different priorities associated with the same or the other in an associated relation between freedom and justice. On the one hand, the acts of comprehension or cognition that operate within ontology are taken by Levinas to exemplify the unfettered *freedom* that self-identification gives itself in its reduction of the other. Again, he locates this tendency inside philosophy itself, running all the way from the ideal of Socratic truth down to the exercise of existential grasping in Heidegger. On the other hand, a critique of this philosophy of power introduces for Levinas the notion of *justice* as one which fundamentally underpins an ethical relation with the other.

A double focus on language and justice now dominates the rest of *Totality and Infinity*'s first section. Levinas first evokes a Platonic world where knowledge is identified with vision, or a Heideggerian world where truth is disclosure, and observes how in each case an 'economy' of the same turns the other into a theme, and silences it. Against this silencing, then, Levinas celebrates the revelation of the Other that takes place in expression, in true discourse (as opposed to mere rhetoric), in conversation and in teaching. For Levinas, this amounts to more than the idea of intersubjectivity. He emphasizes how I am ethically called upon to respond in the linguistic relation with the other, and how the absolute experience of a true face-to-face conversation breaks open the closed monologue of the same, and so introduces transcendence. In this way, transcendence is actually inherently social and plural in Levinas, rather than something isolated or sacred, and indeed, it can be quite intimately related to the establishment and maintenance of justice. The other's revelation to me in expression is therefore regarded by Levinas as the first event of ethics.

ENJOYMENT AND THE FEMININE

In contrast to the task of living in Heidegger, with its stress on manipulation, building and maintenance, Levinas is clear that life is first and foremost experienced as a love of life. As he puts it, the bare fact of life is never bare (TI 112), since from the beginning it is full of the stuff that makes life enjoyable. In the course of his analysis here, Levinas engagingly points to a whole set of tools that are social and even hedonistic: the cigarette lighter, the fork or the cup. They are intentionally the opposite of the whole Heideggerian toolkit that would be used in building and dwelling, not just in being social rather than somehow solitary, or used in pursuit of enjoyment, rather than as part of some heroic labour, but also in the way they represent the confirmation of intimate relationships with something other than being within 'the very pulsation of the I' (TI 113).

Levinas then develops this contrast, by pitting the notions of labour and possession which he associates with Heideggerian dwelling, against a vision of the home as a place of enjoyment, of familiarity and intimacy, of welcome and respite. The home can act as an invitation rather than as a protective exclusion. The contrast is mildly extreme, but it is really designed to operate as an ethical vision. Heideggerian metaphors of building and dwelling contain within them, in Levinas's view, a philosophy of anonymous reality and a solitary self-establishment and possession; whereas for Levinas, reality from the beginning involves a welcoming of the other. In Levinas's social and ethical vision, then, dwelling and language, are not about imposing, grasping and founding. Instead, they exemplify how the self begins in hospitality, and recognizes the other in a way that amounts to 'a primordial dispossession, a first donation' (TI 173).

However, Levinas's characterization of hospitality at this point also gives rise to new problems, for in uprooting the notion of home, he chooses to personalize its moral ethos as *la Femme*, i.e. Woman or Wife. Levinas clearly wishes to give a vision of dwelling that contrasts completely with the image of a hut in the forest inhabited by a solitary male, which is stereotypically associated with Heidegger's philosophical meditations. But Levinas's consequent stress on intimacy, discretion and gentleness starts in turn to produce an ambiguous representation when he centres his vision approvingly on the 'silent comings and goings of the feminine being' (TI 156). That is to say, Levinas identifies the other 'who welcomes in intimacy' as having specifically a feminine alterity, one which is moreover 'situated on another plane than language', displays 'discretion' and can be 'reserved' (TI 155). For all the contextual point of this gendered dynamics, the cameo itself situates woman as the handmaid to an implicitly masculine effort of expression. She seems, in other words, to serve the possibilities of the face-to-face relation and of language without taking on these activities herself or even being invited to do so. This ambiguity has the effect of further raising the stakes for the most fundamental and dramatic emblem in *Totality and Infinity*: the face.

ETHICS AND THE FACE

The *face* embodies all of Levinas's aims in *Totality and Infinity*. Though the face is intimately linked to sensibility and vision in an ordinary sense, and also for Levinas in philosophical experience, the face, in its isolated significance here, now emerges as the emblem of everything that fundamentally resists categorization, containment or comprehension. Levinas therefore describes it as being 'infinitely foreign' (TI 194) or as manifesting the Other's inviolability and holiness. But we are not talking here about the face in a biological, ethnic or even social sense. The face evoked is rather the concrete appearance of the idea of infinity that exists within me. Once again, Levinas develops this ethical image against a background of Western philosophy, which he claims has given a largely negative or presupposed significance to infinity. The idea of infinity which the face encapsulates is for Levinas the key means by which thought is brought into relation with what goes beyond its capacity. And Levinas terms this situation the 'welcome of the face' (TI 197). So the face ethically fulfils the whole purpose of Levinas's philosophy, in the way it is perceived to resist possession or utilization, and for Levinas invites and obliges me to take on a responsibility that transcends knowledge. If the face does promote a discourse when it invites me, though, Levinas is clear that such a discourse arrives with all the force of the fundamental commandment 'Thou shalt not kill'. In other words, this face clearly and incontestably signifies an absolute ethical knowledge which is there from the beginning.

As the significance of the face is there from the beginning, and is non-negotiable, Levinas is also clear that it actually predicts any mystical, liturgical or artful presentation of its message. Indeed, he goes so far as to say that prose, not poetry, is the appropriately sober means of communication. There is a problem here for Levinas which we examine in detail later, when looking at his appreciations of the artwork. And it is a claim that surely sits uneasily with the occasional excesses and opacities of Levinas's own linguistic efforts. But what he is stressing here crucially is that our response to what the face exposes as an ethical demand cannot be mediated or interpreted by us prior to accepting the message. Instead, the face obliges us to receive the idea of infinity prior to engaging the operations of cognition. This can sound impossible: how can we receive an idea prior to entering ideas? For Levinas, though, this is logical. It is the ethical import of language itself that is its meaning. As a result, Levinas also presents the face-to-face situation as one that actually founds language, for it is the face that brings about the very first signification. And in the same way, this founding face also signifies the existence already of a fundamental pluralism. Others exist before me.

This last idea brings back the notion of justice. The way in which the face, revealed to me, obligates me, in the light of infinity, means that justice also emerges from this first moment fully formed as a non-negotiable responsibility. But there can also be a problem attached to this view of the infinity and pre-existence of justice. It is hard not to think of the idea of infinity, its revelation in the face and the transcendence of cognition as having theological resonances, even if Levinas here cautiously tries to play down this thought. For example, when Levinas once again recalls Descartes's Third Meditation, and specifically its conclusion that only the idea of a being more perfect than myself, within me, can make me know my imperfections, Levinas describes the text's contemplation of the Divine majesty as 'the expression of this transformation of the idea of infinity conveyed by knowledge into Majesty approached as a face' (TI 212). We have to recognize how Levinas's choice of words translates and effectively transforms Descartes's reference to God into the Levinasian emblem. Similarly, at the end of the section entitled 'The Other and the

Others' (*Autrui et les Autres*), where Levinas speaks of 'a command that commands commanding' and describes the discourse inherent in the relation with the other as a sermon, an exhortation and a prophetic word (TI 213), he effectively links the fraternity within the idea of infinity to monotheism (TI 214). These connections inevitably make Levinas's absolute and primary justice more culturally localized. Levinas himself is all too aware of how religious references may create a trap for his ethical position, which could be then dismissed philosophically as piety. This is one reason why he stresses the human dimension of the relationship. As he puts it at the very beginning of the next section, alluding to the religious philosopher Kierkegaard, the 'presence of the face coming from beyond the world, but committing me to human fraternity, does not overwhelm me as a numinous essence arousing fear and trembling. To be in relationship while absolving oneself from this relation is to speak' (TI 215). So Levinas is anxious to ensure that the face will at no point be reabsorbed into a venerated representation of the face. This is because the summons that Levinas feels comes to me from the face must not and cannot be discharged by any set response, including one that is theological. The face in the end always speaks directly and absolutely to me, and my acknowledgement, in Levinas's scenario, must equally be absolutely personal.

SØREN AABYE KIERKEGAARD (1813–55)

Danish philosopher and theologian, often presented as a founder of existentialism. Rejecting the Hegelian system of dialectics as an attempt to replace God with man, that ignores the subjective and incomplete nature of all judgement, Kierkegaard emphasizes the anguish, ignorance and wilful nature of all knowledge, in such books as the 1843 works *Fear and Trembling* and *Either/Or*, the 1846 *Concluding Unscientific Postscript* and the 1849 *The Sickness unto Death*. Logically, his books can contradict each another, and some were even produced under invented names so that he could attack them. His influence grew in the twentieth century and especially during the inter-war years as existentialists pondered contemporary ethical choices in a time of uncertainty.

EROS AND FECUNDITY

The face is not actually contained by form or image, even if it manifests itself concretely before me. This means that its ethics could in principle be exemplified by any other part of the body. However, the face-to-face relation is not really just a dramatic embodiment of infinity for Levinas. In truth, it also usefully gives an idealized presentation of an erotic dimension. In a way, the face also signifies for Levinas as a means of *not* fixating on other body parts. One example of how this is so occurs when Levinas refers to the face of the *Beloved*. The Beloved is quite precisely someone who is 'graspable but intact in her nudity, beyond object and face and thus beyond the existent' (TI 258). The erotic relation immediately becomes the lack of one, as the Beloved is at once presented as something fragile, vulnerable, tender, modest and most tellingly, perhaps, a virgin. In fact, Levinas adds that this 'Eternal Feminine' 'is the virgin or the incessant recommencement of virginity' (TI 258), in other words, a space that in being violated becomes inviolable. While this Beloved is obviously meant to represent an ethical space that forever remains 'ungraspable' by a Heideggerian virility, she also joins a select but growing band of ethical assistants in Levinas's scenarios who offer a gendered embodiment of his ethics that, in a real situation, some would find a claustrophobically traditional and subservient role.

When the Beloved enters or becomes the house of hospitality, moreover, we see how Eros becomes fecundity. In a closing section of *Totality and Infinity*, Levinas moves beyond the erotic relation towards 'the marvel of the family' (TI 306). What this family moreover really seems to encapsulate is transcendence, which is produced through paternity or fecundity, and confirmed by the child. Indeed, we even have to note that the child is more particularly the son. This family naturally does not represent the triumph of biological self-preservation. Rather, it is the place where Levinas locates 'the infinity of paternity' or the 'infinite time' of fecundity. This is an ethical family unit, then, which represents an absolute primary sociality and a rejection of 'the isolated and heroic being that the State produces' (TI 306). On one level, this modest and good family is a fitting and moving end to the massive critique launched in *Totality and Infinity*, and in addition has to be appreciated in the context of the painful post-war re-founding of both real life and a philosophy of existence.

On another level, this closing image of the family is vaguely dis-
appointing in its somewhat conformist and even conservative representation of ethical time and extreme passivity.

PRESENTING THE OTHER

As we have already indicated at several points, the exposition of
Totality and Infinity's ethical vision, with its heavily involved undoing of
ontological language and schemes, generates a tortuous and sometimes
contradictory way of arguing. Some of this is made better by the act
of reading the book, since terms become defined through their repetition or through their evolving relation to one another, and succeeding
sections begin to draw a progressive line through the history of
Western philosophy down to present concerns. And some of it is
made a little worse by the same act of reading, as when we start to
realize that ethical 'undoing' can coalesce in a number of fairly traditional roles. But the work's difficulties arise above all from its fundamental paradox, which is that it tries to present the Other as such, in
a philosophical discourse that, by its very inherited nature, enshrines
the language of the Same.

The earliest and still most powerful exposé of this fundamental
problem is undoubtedly Jacques Derrida's essay on the works by
Levinas running up to and including *Totality and Infinity*, entitled
'Violence and Metaphysics'. This essay initially appeared three years
after Levinas's text, in 1964, before becoming a key chapter in
Derrida's 1967 *Writing and Difference*. It is all the more convincing as a
critique for being respectful of Levinas's text, in part since the fundamental problem articulated by Levinas also went to the heart of
deconstruction's own ambiguous relationship to the Western philosophical tradition. Some of Derrida's reading involves the traditional
academic task of paraphrasing and commenting on the text, while
contradicting certain characterizations, notably of Husserl and Heidegger,
wherein Levinas supposedly 'criticizes the one in a style and according
to a scheme borrowed from the other, and finishes by sending them
off into the wings as partners in the "play of the same" and accomplices in the same historico-philosophical coup' (WD 98). Derrida also
points up inconsistencies, such as the re-introduction of concepts
which Levinas's earlier texts had criticized, as well as emphasizing how
Levinas is closer in his views and sympathies to various philosophical

adversaries than he is prepared to recognize, as with the case of Hegel. But these are merely preludes to the real problem, which is that of 'lodging oneself within traditional conceptuality in order to destroy it' (WD 111), and therefore of presupposing and perpetuating the ontological violence which Levinas's work seeks to oppose and overcome. Derrida devastatingly concludes that '[b]y making the origin of language, meaning, and difference the relation to the infinitely other, Levinas is resigned to betraying his own intentions in his philosophical discourse' (WD 151).

In an oblique response, published only in 1973, Levinas's essay 'Wholly Otherwise' returns the gesture by picking up on the recourse to ontological language in Derrida's own critique. The long delay in replying was of course an intellectual acknowledgement of the criticism's pertinence, and it became obvious from subsequent work that Derrida's assessment of Levinas's position had an important influence, extending beyond just questions of dialogue and inclusivity into a radical re-forming of his work. This influence is most astonishingly discernible in the transformations which Levinas's philosophy undergoes in his next major philosophical publication. This is the 1974 *Otherwise than Being or Beyond Essence*, published just a year after 'Wholly Otherwise'. It is to this most radical and ambitious text by Levinas that we now turn.

SUMMARY

The first of Levinas's two major philosophical works, *Totality and Infinity*, criticizes the totalizing operation of previous philosophical systems in the West, and argues for the priority of an absolute ethics which places us not within totality but within infinity. Key features of this approach are:

- The revelation of the Other.
- The face as an ethical site.
- Femininity and fecundity.
- Infinity.

4

OTHERWISE THAN BEING OR BEYOND ESSENCE

Otherwise than Being or Beyond Essence was published as a book in 1974 but is based on lectures and articles dating back some seven years. It therefore continues with some implications of the major moral programme outlined in *Totality and Infinity*. Here the asymmetrical tensions between Being and Other are presented dramatically through intense phenomenological examinations of our subjectivity, temporality, responsibility and infinitude. Once again, then, Levinas is contesting a vision of Western philosophical closure that he feels culminates in Heideggerian Being. But on another level, *Otherwise than Being* radically disrupts many of the premises still intact within *Totality and Infinity*. This has to do with a number of logical consequences arising from the earlier work, such as its self-defeatingly successful presentation of the unthematizable, as well as the key paradox which Derrida exposed in his lucid critique, concerning how an attempt to undo conceptuality ends up by retaining it. It is in part for these reasons that *Otherwise than Being* can seem such a strangely expressive and even violent text that hardly resembles philosophy at all. This chapter tries to clarify the main ideas of *Otherwise than Being*, works through its difficult language and radical terminology, focuses especially on the issues of saying and passivity, and follows Levinas's subsequent debate with Jacques Derrida about the difficulties and even impossibilities inherent in such a radical project.

LANGUAGE AND ORDER

From the beginning of *Otherwise than Being*, we get a sense of the huge revolutions of language and organization which Levinas is going to undergo, and of the way in which this task will crucially have to involve avoidance, indirection and unsaying. A preliminary note advises that the term 'essence' expresses the German *Sein* (being). Levinas adds that he has not dared to write this as the deconstruction-looking *essance* (though, obviously, writing this is tantamount to putting it in place, in a rather deconstructive manner). Then he writes that the term *essence* is anyway not to be read traditionally, will be carefully avoided as a term and is actually going to be rendered as 'eidos'. Yet, subsequently, this does not happen. We are also told that the work is composed of several previous publications but is, all the same, not a collection of articles, since a first version of the book actually preceded the published texts which were taken out of it and made autonomous. But then these published texts were reintroduced without the changes being effaced, even though subsequent changes were made and more notes were added. And then we are given, in a concise but grammatically inverted sentence, the book's main propositions, which a subsequent remark claims are not original anyway:

> To see [*reconnaître*] in subjectivity an exception [*ex-ception*] putting out of order [*déréglant*] the conjunction of essence [*essence*], entities [*étant*] and the 'difference'; to catch sight [*apercevoir*], in the substantiality of the subject, in the hard core of the 'unique' in me, in my unparalleled [*dépareillée*] identity, of a substitution for the other; to conceive of [*penser*] this abnegation prior to the will [*d'avant le vouloir*] as a merciless exposure to the trauma of transcendence by way of a susception more, and differently, passive than receptivity, passion and finitude; to derive praxis and knowledge in [*intérieurs au*] the world from this nonassumable susceptibility.
>
> (OB xlvii–xlviii)

The English translation cannot adequately give, and even serves to mask or contradict, the tortuous way in which Levinas is here trying to lay forth terms and programmes which look to avoid the problems he now acknowledges to be inherent even in philosophical exposition. Seeing is not recognizing, for example; and the un-doing processes of Levinas's language are not heard or seen so well in the English version.

Before we even enter the book, then, Levinas flags up very complex linguistic and structural effects, which are designed to promote the radical philosophical attempt to truly *think* (and not just conceive) otherwise than 'being' or beyond 'essence'.

As an accompanying part of this revolution, Levinas equally lays earlier key terms such as the Same or Totality rather to one side, and introduces a whole new set of deliberately extreme and disruptive descriptions, such as obsession, hostage and expiation, or else gives violent and upsetting images of subjection, involving skin, lungs, burning, flesh, wounds and trauma. In fact, words themselves are made to suffer in this book: they are snapped apart and hyphenated, as in *ex-ception* or *re-tain*; or they are edgily re-peated and re-turned and re-inforced, as when he writes 'we say that they *are* beyond essence, that is, that beyond essence *they are*' (OB 29); or they are composed into mutant non-categories like the 'one-penetrated-by-the-other'; or they are endlessly re-defined and re-voiced to the point where a stream of thought actually collapses, as when we get 'from the first a "me who ... ," but in fact "me who am known to you," "me whose voice you find in your memories," or "me who could situate myself in the system of your history"' (OB 27). This last example rather brilliantly enacts its own message about the pre-original and undefinable commanding voice of ethics, by the way in which it is taken over linguistically, and the self-assertion becomes endlessly deferred and opened up to an infinitude of obligations and responsibilities. Some of Levinas's sentences now also emerge with no verb at all, while others become distended or delayed, in a form of de-mastering. In a similar fashion, the book's general architecture overturns or distorts some of Levinas's earlier approaches: the argument now, which is focused on subjectivity rather than alterity, proceeds less via grand organizational stratifications like Same and Other, Interiority and Exteriority, which retain at least implicitly a linearity, than through a more vulnerable, immediate and obsessive prose that painfully lives and embodies its own evocations of suffering, exposure and inspiration, and in its relationship with the reader accepts its own 'invitation to the fine risk of approach qua approach' (OB 94).

The violence done to both the text and to concepts here is clearly meant to be an intellectual acknowledgement of the paradox inherent in *Totality and Infinity*'s metaphysics, which was exposed by Derrida's essay 'Violence and Metaphysics'. But it is also conceivably another version of the recollection of war, as evoked at the beginning of *Totality and Infinity*. Here, though, we could say that *Otherwise than Being* is so conscious of the paradox of thematization that it strives instead to be a de-thematized enactment of suffering and dereliction in general, and of the Shoah and the Second World War in particular. This view would be supported by the prefatory epigraphs. First, in French, Levinas writes: 'To the memory of those who were closest among the six million assassinated by the National Socialists, and of the millions on millions of all confessions and all nations, victims of the same hatred of the other man, the same anti-Semitism' (OB v). Levinas's wording carefully indicates how the work's memory is both of loved ones and of unknown and unnamed millions, how its historical consciousness is informed by the fate both of Jews in the Shoah and of all victims of hatred, and how its ethical exposure is one in which the upsurge of anti-Semitism during the war period betokens a fundamental hatred of the other. This general sense of testimony, which remains implicit rather than explicit throughout most of the book, but where we could say that the whole book bears witness to it, also contributes to a need to bring the notions of expression and language explored in *Totality and Infinity* into something much more urgent and transformative. This is in part conveyed by the subsequent epigraph, written this time in Hebrew, where Levinas dedicates the work to his family, all of whom with one exception were victims of the Holocaust: his father, Yekhiel ben Rabbi Avraham Halevi; his mother, Dvora bat Rabbi Moshe Halevi; his brothers, Dov ben Rabbi Yehiel and Aminadav ben Rabbi Yekhiel Halevi; his father-in-law, Shmuel ben Rabbi Gershon Halevi; and his mother-in-law, Malki bat Rabbi Haim. With this act of naming and of general remembrance, the themes of experience may be supported but they are also outreached by a fundamental gesture of saying and un-saying. A saying that is simultaneously an un-saying is enacted in order to rupture the residual certainties of philosophical language and structure, and so to bring thought perhaps into the unmasterable domain of devotion. The force of this particular *saying* is therefore what Levinas now examines.

THE SAID AND THE SAYING

One of the key messages and lessons of *Otherwise than Being* has to do with the actual ethical force of *saying*. Levinas here comes close to paraphrasing Derrida's critique of *Totality and Infinity* regarding the subjugation of *saying* as a gesture to the finality and immobility of the *said*:

> Is not the inescapable fate in which being immediately includes the statement of being's *other* not due to the hold that the *said* has over the *saying*, to the *oracle* in which the said is immobilized? Then would not the bankruptcy of transcendence be but that of a theology that thematizes the *transcending* in the logos ... ?
>
> (OB 5)

At once, Levinas starts to elaborate the alternative, that is, to emphasize how saying, before it conjugates a verbal sign, is already an ethical gesture. Saying is therefore already 'the proximity of one to the other, the commitment of an approach, the one for the other, the very signifyingness of signification' (OB 5). However, rather than accept next that the purity of saying's intentions will inevitably be compromised and subordinated once saying enters into the service of the said, that is, the thematization of being, Levinas insists that verbalization does not exhaust the *signifyingness* of saying. Instead, a philosophy of otherwise than being can raise the game, precisely by elaborating a new 'saying that must also be unsaid' (OB 7). In this stubborn and devotional gesture, we can try to free the bird of transcendence from the cage of thematics. Moreover, ethical saying logically has to carry on doing this in a forever unresolved manner. What this now produces in Levinas is a perpetually unfurling thought, a kind of temporal pulsing movement that continues to resist collapsing into a settled expression.

This aspiration will set the strictly impossible terms for the rest of the work's manifestation of responsibility for the other, for logically this mission can be even adequately expressed only through a certain impossible undoing of language. As Levinas puts it at one point, we somehow have to generate a 'saying saying saying itself' (OB 143), if we are to overcome the paradoxes inherent in presenting a philosophical other. The phrase bears out once again the temporalization of Being, and the need somehow not to defer to a past, or a representation, or an ordering that predates and therefore in a way predetermines the situation of ethical thought. In fact, what at first glance had perhaps seemed like a scrambled framework and a tangled language now start to look like very careful and exemplary constructions, since it is exactly the enigmatic and equivocating nature of saying that Levinas presents as the actual means to express responsibility for the other and the precedence of the other, without effectively suppressing them in the process. In other words, the task of producing a saying that defines my subjectivity's presence and place becomes infinitely renewable from second to second. Moreover, I cannot just freely take on this task of being responsible for the other. Rather, my subjectivity is located only within this perpetually restated responsibility for the other. As Levinas carefully demonstrates, it is therefore more accurate to situate my subjectivity linguistically and ethically in a non-presence and a non-place (OB 10).

This task creates extreme conditions of subjection for saying. In seeking to undo the distance and mastery which we construct with the said, saying becomes totally exposed in its approach to the other. In limited social situations, this creates the risk, at least, of embarrassment or rebuttal, and at worst, perhaps, of sounding psychotic. But in this philosophical context, Levinas needs to present ethical exposure as being absolute and excessive, something that will strip away all protective layers, whether cultural or literal, from the body (of knowledge). Thus he presents saying here as a situation that first of all turns us into a skin that can be wounded or a cheek that can be struck. But this kind of denuding is then immediately recognized to be just the prelude to its full ethical consequence. Since saying is here viewed as the signifyingness of our definitive exile from the haven of thematization, it becomes not just a moment of exposure, but in itself the expression of exposure as such. Therefore, Levinas calls it 'a denuding of denuding', meaning that saying has to carry on being saying. It can never rest, having said what it has to say. Instead, saying is permanently torn from itself.

Now an obvious problem with this extreme presentation of saying, of course, is that it so absolutely tries to counteract the power and repressiveness of the said, or the violence of ontology itself, that it starts to exert its own violence. The being-for-the-other testified to by this extreme ethical saying can come to sound like a masochistic scenario that confers humiliation and real pain on the subject. In fact, when Levinas evokes the trauma of absolute saying, and presents the vulnerability and passivity of this position in a bodily way, he conjures up quasi-sexual scenarios of subordination, where ethical being is for example one-penetrated-by-the-other (OB 49). The suggestion of sexual positions here, in conjunction with visions of maternity and femininity elsewhere, can evoke extremity is a way that seems problematically to gender a philosophy of the other. In speaking, for example, of labour pains (OB 51) as well as the patience of corporeality, Levinas may well be offering, even subconsciously, an absolute contrast to contemporary developments in French feminism. In April 1971, this had been marked by publication of a manifesto provocatively entitled the 'Manifesto of the 343 Bitches', in which the signatories (including the philosopher Simone de Beauvoir) admitted to having had an illegal abortion and asserted that 'our bellies belong to us'. The same year equally saw the formation of the pro-abortion group Choice (*Choisir*) which lobbied for contraception and free abortion on demand. These facilities finally passed into law in France in two phases, at the end of 1974, the year of publication of *Otherwise than Being*, and again in January 1975. So Levinas's 'otherwise' in this context can perhaps also be read as not speaking, and even indirectly contradicting, these parallel reformist discourses. We can return to this point, but for now at least we can note that the self experiencing Levinas's form of extreme giving is evicted from the secure place of the ego, and that although it is devoted to the other, it is logically not even able to decide to be devoted, since such a decision would in itself entail a self-possession or a self-positioning. Such a radical servitude therefore means that we have to ask what kind of actual subjectivity we can find in such a saying. In order to evoke this extreme kind of subjectivity, Levinas introduces two key, radical modes of ethical consciousness that live out a non-erotic, non-thematized and non-liberating commitment to the other: namely, *proximity* and *obsession*.

PROXIMITY AND OBSESSION

For Levinas, humanity *is* proximity. But crucially, it is primarily rather than secondarily so. That is to say, we are not talking about first having consciousness, and then a negotiation with other persons and things. Instead, proximity arrives first. In fact, proximity is not really a relationship between two terms at all for Levinas, since that would establish, in however indirect a manner, some sort of synchronizing between the same and the other. Proximity, for Levinas, is fundamentally non-reciprocal and occurs before we get any thematization. He says that it involves instead 'the very establishing of the-one-for-the-other' (OB 85). This is another case, then, of existing *exceptionally*, of finding ourselves in a non-space where our relations are based not on a system but on an already urgent and unsatisfiable obligation. We might well argue that such an 'anarchic' notion of humanity would be politically unworkable and probably quite scandalous. But in Levinas's ethical scenarios this is exactly what humanity, as opposed to mere *condition*, truly is. Once again there are contemporary intellectual, social and political differences alluded to here. What he indirectly contradicts is a general series of philosophies of humanity based on the 'dogmatism of mathematical and dialectical relations' (OB 58) or the calculated suspicions of psychoanalysis, sociology and politics (OB 59). Levinas's view of politics and society, at least as he claims it here, is grounded in a primary and never surpassed concern for the neighbour, to whom I am connected by an original and non-contractual bond. My proximity to this 'neighbour' (OB 85) is not arrived at by a logical or legal or even merely conventional process. Instead, there is a primary command that establishes this proximity, a preconditional non-indifference to the neighbour, who is defined not geographically or biologically, but morally. The neighbour is therefore already all of humanity, prior to the introduction of society, or even subjectivity. So the term proximity indicates something excessive for Levinas. It signifies a community that exists before any established fact, where the other's singularity is experienced by me as unparalleled, overwhelming, extreme, exclusive and pre-assigned. There is simply no choice in the matter.

This complete and uncalculating proximity, where I am in total service to the other without even the thought of service arising, has earlier been linked by Levinas to the state of maternity. But in a more edgy evocation of a relation that has no borders or breaks in it, he now calls it an *obsession*. Levinas's descriptions renew once more the extreme and uneasy nature of this answerability, in the way they almost suggest social taboos: self-exposure, touching without consummation, persecution. Being-for-the-other here, which is one-way, unsatisfiable and unreciprocated, suddenly sounds like a kind of moral stalking. What Levinas presumably wishes to evoke is how the proximity he is describing is not a relationship based on consciousness or knowing. But he is also deliberately looking to generate an obsessive ethical *language*. Given what he takes proximity to be, his own philosophical language cannot remain just within a socially comfortable realm, but rather has to generate its own de-thematization. Obsession, then, necessarily produces instances of Levinas obsessively voicing obsession, as when he writes, for example: 'prior to all reflection, prior to every positing, an indebtedness before any loan, not assumed, anarchical, subjectivity of a bottomless passivity, made out of assignation, like the echo of a sound that would precede the resonance of this sound' (OB 111). This is not normal philosophical – or even social – language, but that is just the point: it exactly expresses the passive and pre-dialogic nature of obsession and the absolute ethical responsibility that it is trying impossibly to manifest. In other words, it gives in its own obsessive exposition a sense of that persecuted subjectivity which Levinas is presenting as ethical being, a subjectivity that is hostage to the other even in its verbal existence. It exists, even linguistically, as an endless process of substitution.

SUBSTITUTION AND JUSTICE

Substitution is the key term of *Otherwise than Being*, and the chapter that exposes it is the work's centrepiece. It has to be said at once that the context of the chapter's original appearance in 1968 makes Levinas's descriptions of anarchy, solidarity, commitment, fraternity, manifestation and communication all stand out as terms that are fundamentally and consciously different from their usage in contemporary social revolt. In addition, negative references to Sartre, Hegel or Eugen Fink (who was Husserl's assistant), as well as a closing reference to '[m]odern antihumanism' (OB 127), again are meant to reflect a barely tacit disagreement regarding the absolute responsibility of freedom, which does not here rely or rest on any individual commitment to a cause. Encapsulating and even surpassing the other terms we have already encountered, *substitution* is presented by Levinas as being a passivity beyond even passivity, or an absolutely extreme 'possibility of every sacrifice for the other' (OB 115). There is, of course, no notion of compulsion or recompense or even of alienation suggested as an underlying reason. Instead, Levinas again recalls religious transcendence (though he is clear that this appeal remains outside of any mysticism) by speaking of how substitution is *inspired*. Levinas localizes this emptying-out of identity, linguistically and religiously, when he specifies that '[t]he word *I* means *here I am*' (OB 114). The total and constant responsiveness that *here I am* evokes relies, naturally, on the entire biblical series of replies to the Lord, including most obviously that of Abraham (Genesis 22: 1) and of Samuel (I Samuel 3: 4), while the actual French phrase '[l]e mot *je* signifie *me voici*' enacts in itself a dislocation of the *I* from the nominative *je* to the accusative *me*. At the same moment, Levinas introduces the equally challenging notion of being hostage (and later even martyr) to the other, in further emphasis of the non-volition of this state, and in a manner that also generally recalls a biblical devotion to a higher cause. And yet we must not imagine that being a hostage or a substitute here has to involve a dramatic act any more than it entails a free gesture. In fact, Levinas even locates substitution at one point in the deliberately banal and bourgeois phrase 'After you'. So substitution can be a near-invisible event, which is almost ironic, given the massive inversion of priorities which it symbolizes as having taken place in Levinas's own work, between *Totality and Infinity* and *Otherwise than Being.* While the earlier work's critique still focused primarily on transcendence and its conscious philosophical scenarios of encounter with the other, the later work now largely envisages concrete and non-philosophical situations, where an already internalized spirit is to be manifested without will or consciousness, like a bearing witness. This is what leads Levinas to say that substitution is not a psychological event, or compassion, or 'intropathy' (OB 146), for nothing is actually taken on. The phrase 'After you', like 'here I am', is chosen in order to empha-size how substitution, far from being a statement of knowledge or commitment, bears witness, or gives voice in the tiniest of moments, and despite oneself, to the Infinite. So substitution, for Levinas, is actually related quite intimately to both subjectivity and saying, since infinity, in Levinas's scenario, becomes 'an inwardness in the sincerity of a witness borne', and since, as a witness, it commands me by my own mouth or 'orders me by my own voice' (OB 147).

This dimension of bearing witness, in substitution, could easily be thought of as prophetic in tone. But just as important for Levinas is the fact that it acknowledges a fundamental sense of *justice*. That is to say, substitution involves acknowledging that I am answerable to all rather than to just one. And this is therefore a concern with justice. This justice, of course, is precisely not law, and is even the opposite of it, at the level of ethical saying as opposed to the juridical said. The problem here is that, inevitably, the promotion of justice for all must involve the introduction of thematization, and the imposition of a said onto a pure anarchic saying. Nonetheless, Levinas feels that justice is born of the same primary witnessing. He cites Isaiah 57: 19: 'Peace, peace, to the far and to the near' (where his French version helps the point along by placing *prochain* or the near, before *lointain* or the far), in order to emphasize, prophetically, how intimate proximity and a more general contiguity or being-together, are not separate. In this way, *Otherwise than Being* concludes much more powerfully than did *Totality and Infinity* (where it was more a question of plurality) when it comes to seeing the necessity of justice as being the actual foundation of consciousness, as well as seeing how a de-situated *I*, in an unrequited relationship with the other, is also necessary to real justice. In this sense, significantly, there is for Levinas an acceptable thematization and a resolution of saying in the said. It occurs legitimately when everything 'shows itself' and is said in being for justice' (OB 163).

OTHERWISE THAN READING

The task of reading the traumatic and prophetic *Otherwise than Being* is difficult and, for some, it is ultimately a frustrating and vain exercise. The way in which language and conceptuality are pushed to the point of collapse can make it appear as though its ethical aims are self-defeating, or even *merely* obsessive. The introduction of a more messianic tone, and a set of core religious references, can also make some readers feel that we have left philosophy. Certainly, this is no longer philosophy or even ethics in the sense in which they are generally understood by either 'analytic' traditions or even many 'French' philosophers. But the difficulty of reading this work relates ultimately not to ways in which it merely fails, but to the fact that it quite deliberately fails certain demands. It does this precisely in order to be faithful to its most radical point, which is that we are obligated ethically to the surpassing of categorical constraints.

The possibility of reading *Otherwise than Being* in a manner that manages to be otherwise than just reading, if you like, is encouraged by Levinas himself, in his own eventual acknowledgement of the force of Derrida's reading of his work. The result, 'Wholly Otherwise', was first published in a 1973 edition of the journal *L'Arc* dedicated to the work of Derrida. It therefore predates the publication of *Otherwise than Being*, but postdates the appearance in extract form of that book's various parts, which is one straightforward reason why Levinas can refer at the essay's end to 'a contact made in the heart of a chiasmus' (WO 8) with Derrida's thinking. The essay, with its more limited confines and address, gives a sharper view of how the transcending language of *Otherwise than Being*, far from being merely delirious, has grown in large measure quite logically out of the endless task of reading responsibly, or as we might say, following Levinas, of reading reading reading itself. Levinas's essay opens with a potentially paternalistic recognition of Derrida's 'new style of thinking' (WO 3), its *frisson* or literary effect (WO 4), and its pyrotechnic aspirations to show that we are perhaps, again, 'at the end of a naïveté, of an unsuspected dogmatism [, a] new break in the history of philosophy' (WO 3). It also notably refers not to Derrida's 1964 essay on Levinas, 'Violence and Metaphysics', but only explicitly to his 1967 *Voice and Phenomenon*. This is probably his most purely phenomenological work and certainly the most traditional and austere of the three books that Derrida astonishingly published that same year, the others being *Writing and Difference* (which contains 'Violence and Metaphysics') and *Of Grammatology*. Levinas's opening section, entitled 'It's today tomorrow', also concludes with a rather ambiguous joke that explains the title, about a half-drunk barber who, during the Nazi occupation of France, offers to shave soldiers for free, a joke that plays on the French phrase *demain on rase gratis* (literally 'Free shaves tomorrow', that is to say, never, since tomorrow always remains tomorrow). Levinas comments in an obvious reference to deconstruction's *différance* that the barber's action symbolically gave us an 'essential procrastination – the future *différance* – … reabsorbed into the present', before suggesting once again ambiguously that the barber perhaps was just raving, 'as delirious as that fourth form of delirium described in the *Phaedrus*, in which, since Plato, the disclosure of Western metaphysics has remained' (WO 4). In other words, philosophy's pretension to break free of the history of philosophy is perhaps deluded, just drunk on its own poetry and blind to its real historical situation. (We can also hear, yet again, the denunciation of Heidegger.)

And yet, Levinas's remarks here are already moving subtly towards intellectual proximity. For this delirium, we soon realize, is not something that Levinas presents as existing just in a break in the history of philosophy. Instead, it is actually already there at the very heart of Western philosophy's metaphysical *disclosure* of the truth of being.

So if Derrida manifests delirious ambition, it is inevitably shared by Levinas himself. The deprecating introduction actually gestures towards philosophical proximity. In the guise of commenting on Derrida's *Voice and Phenomenon*, Levinas then articulates a philosophical messianism that in effect outlines the course of his own *Otherwise than Being*, and in the process locates (in a language and an approach of dis-location) the radicality of that still-future work within their 'philoso-phical encounter'. Thus, the earlier image of a defeated France in 1940 (shared here initially between two Jewish philosophers born outside France) becomes remarkably transformed, via an evocation of 'the security of European peoples, behind their frontiers and the walls of their houses, assured of their property' (WO 4). This carries another Heideggerian contestation, for the defeat, or failure, now becomes represented as exemplary. That is to say, philosophy *is* defeat, in the sense that it should be, in Levinas's eyes, 'a defection from an impos-sible presence' (WO 4). This is what Levinas was working towards in *Otherwise than Being*. And it is similarly *philosophical* foundations and edifications, walls and dwellings, that Derrida also 'dismantles or deconstructs' (WO 4) in Levinas's view. This is, moreover, a project 'whose accomplishment is always impossible and which is always deferred' (WO 4), that is to say, one which also introduces a new temporality, as did that moment of defeat and Nazi occupation which marked 'the end or the interim period of France' (WO 4).

The linkages and inversions established here, in a supposedly silly joke, between philosophical and political totality are astonishingly complex, and create a resonant alliance between Levinas and Derrida that obviously goes beyond logical or intellectual collegiality. The 'defection from presence' which is being registered here is then linked to a 'defection from the true', that is to say to a *positive* admission of 'significations which do not have to comply with the summation of Knowledge' (WO 5). This new idea is also incidentally introduced via a most provocative use of allusions to the occupation of France: thus we are given a 'deportation' of Knowledge, and a 'bankrupt' way of life for Being, before a new system of signs, 'a language guided by no full meaning', is 'liberated' (WO 5). Obviously understanding the term *différance* now to be a Derridean description of this newly liberated language, Levinas also turns the tables somewhat, by pointing up how in the wake of deconstruction's liberating effects one is still left with the 'stern architecture' of deconstruction itself, which after all still uses the present tense of the verb 'to be'! And he then follows this by emphasizing his own development of the diachronic and non-simultaneous relation between Saying and Said, which will form the basis of *Otherwise than Being*'s disruptive expressivity and will attempt to give us, as he puts it here, 'a glimpse of these interstices of Being where this very reflection unsays itself' (WO 6). It is in such a 'chiasmus', opened up by a saying that unsays within the said, that Levinas from now on locates Derrida's (and his own) critique in an overview here that is massively supported by *Otherwise than Being*, though he adds teasingly that this is something which 'Derrida will probably deny' (WO 6).

This closing invitation to respond is duly honoured by Derrida in his essay 'At This Very Moment in This Work Here I Am', which was produced six years after the publication of *Otherwise than Being*, in 1980. This essay is itself a tour de force of saying and unsaying, and with its full incorporation and prolonged consideration of key Levinasian terms it becomes on occasions impossible to distinguish where the essay's subject ends and its commentary begins. Derrida tries to offer both a radical acknowledgement (as in the repetition of *here I am*) and a necessary 'radical ingratitude' (AT 15), and to bring these together as a profound disturbance of sovereignty; while the moment, the work, the locus and the identity that are indicated in the essay's title gradually emerge as the concrete situation of an unending ethical encounter. Two related moments of special note occur at the essay's end which all the same mark a particular *différance*. Derrida first introduces and voices the question of alterity as sexual difference which, as we have already seen at several moments, can suggest limits even to the Levinasian wholly other. And he closes by exposing the textual and generic boundaries that are *still* assumed by Levinas's prose, when his own text changes into a largely unpunctuated and capitalized poetic delirium, out of which emerges traces of Levinasian ethics, together with unresolved emotions and encrypted secrets. As ever, Derrida is able to develop a critique of philosophy from within the philosophy itself, and here as elsewhere he is precise in his focus on areas of potential shortcoming. Taking our cue in particular now from the way in which Derrida's closing point isolates how the artistic potential of language and representation can encapsulate Levinasian ethics while indicating an important limit-point in Levinas, it is to Levinas's views on the artwork that we can now turn our attention.

SUMMARY

The second of Levinas's two major philosophical works, *Otherwise than Being or Beyond Essence*, recognizes limits still implicit in the moral vision of *Totality and Infinity*, and addresses these by moving towards a radical restatement of ethical relations. Key features of this approach are:

- The emphasis on Saying rather than the Said.
- Proximity and Obsession as ways of being in relation.
- Substitution and Hostage as radical forms of being-for-the-other.
- Justice.

5

THE ARTWORK

> Art is the pre-eminent exhibition [*ostension*] in which the said is reduced to a pure theme, to absolute exposition [*exposition*], even to shamelessness [*impudeur*] capable of holding all looks for which it is exclusively destined. The said is reduced to the Beautiful, which supports Western ontology.
>
> (OB 40)

This sweeping statement from *Otherwise than Being*, which epitomizes a persistently negative reaction in many of Levinas's writings, seems to condemn any artwork in advance. But as we shall see, Levinas's approach is progressively far more complex than this rigid dismissal might immediately suggest. In this chapter, I shall try to outline Levinas's general vision of the artwork, detail certain dominating influences, read his reaction to key works or writers and point out the important changes and residual tensions in his positions.

VISIONS OF REPRESENTATION

In interviews, Levinas has credited key artworks with giving him a good apprenticeship in philosophical thinking, and he has from the beginning used certain literary texts and authors as well as those of a philosophical canon when formulating absolutely fundamental concepts. On this level at least, Shakespeare has the same status as Plato.

Moreover, this is not just a case of Levinas using literature to illustrate philosophical truths; instead, at key moments in Levinas it is literature that initiates a fundamental dialogue. In other words, contradicting his own statement above, Levinas uses *certain* artworks to open up onto-logical language and philosophical tradition to transcendence. At a certain level of sophistication, where what starts to emerge is a writ-ing whose formal and rhetorical transgressions can help to evoke a practice that can teach philosophy how to go further, the artwork can be recognized by Levinas, and exploited in the task of breaking open philosophy's totality. But this appreciation can peculiarly co-exist, especially in his earlier writings, with an almost impatient censuring of any artwork that Levinas views as just facilitating containment or bearing false witness. In other words, Levinas is prone to praising art when it seems to him to be ethical, and to condemning it if he regards it as a graven image. It is obvious, then, that a highly complex view of the artwork exists in Levinas, one which is actually sometimes just at odds with itself. One way of beginning to understand why this is so, before we start to observe how his critical views evolved and changed, is to review some of the founding influences on Levinas's general assessment of the artwork. There are perhaps three main fields of such influence, deriving from Platonic, Jewish and Heideggerian understandings of art.

PLATO

Plato is a key referent in all of Levinas's writings, not least in terms of a constant recollection of the Platonic notion of the 'Good beyond Being'. Book 10 of Plato's *Republic* had famously dismissed the art of representation as something devoid of serious value since it offers apparitions (or spectres) rather than the truth, can give us no clue as to the goodness or badness of things represented and at best presents something beautifully ill-informed. For Plato, the poet discourages deliberation, encourages unreasoning and makes us fall under a spell. Though Levinas will effectively take issue elsewhere with aspects of Plato's *Republic*, such as the ideal of fusion or the subordination of the feminine (TO 93), which is itself interesting in the light of certain figurations of femininity in his own work, he obviously draws approvingly on Plato's negative judgement here at several points. The best-known (and in terms of stern moralizing, arguably the worst) concrete example of this influence is Levinas's uncompromising assertion of the primacy of philosophical criticism in 'Reality and its Shadow'. First published in 1948 in the existentialist journal *Les Temps Modernes*, this essay was extraordinarily prefaced there by a riposte representing the views of the journal's editorial committee. This preface points out sharply how Levinas omits (or perhaps ignores) what Jean-Paul Sartre had already written of the image in *L'Imaginaire*, and how painting and poetry are also shown to operate beneath the level of the concept in Sartre's contemporary *Situations II*. Ignoring the question of minor rivalries within French phenomenology, it is a little ironic that Levinas is criticized here for failing to discuss the *philosophical* image when the main thrust of his article, which champions 'philosophical criticism', lambasts the dangerous substitution of image for object, and, through that, intelligible object, or concept. Levinas is arguably returning to the very origin of the philosophical image in the way he clearly refers to Plato by stating that art 'lets go of the prey for the shadow' (LR 141), 'the beautiful of modern art [is] opposed to the happy beauty of classical art' (LR 141) and 'the poet exiles himself from the city [since] art is not the supreme value of civilization' (LR 142). In contrast, it is precisely philosophical exegesis and criticism (which he half-heartedly admits can be found in modern literature) that Levinas sees as challenging 'artistic idolatry' in order to re-introduce the world of illusions and shadows to 'the intelligible world [which is] the true homeland of the mind' (LR 142).

This last reference also lets us see, though, how this apparently Platonic position is more pointedly an attempt to link artistic irresponsibility to a nationalist and specifically Heideggerian landscape. In the context of Plato's *Republic*, Levinas's remarks are also here intended as an opposition to Heidegger, and specifically to the latter's 1931–32 lectures on the Cave Allegory, published as *The Essence of Truth*. These had emphasized among other things the symbolic centrality of visuality to knowledge and the corruption of fundamental meanings by ethics, together with the inherent role of *aletheia* or truth as 'dis-closure'. I shall return to this dimension in a minute. For now we can see, though, that the editorial committee's criticism of Levinas's philosophical ignorance is correct in one unintended sense. What is astonishing in 'Reality and its Shadow' is a derogatory use of terms that will actually become positive and indeed crucial in the mature philosophy of *Otherwise than Being*. Here, though, they are used to designate how art remains trapped in obscurity and, as an instance of the *there is*, in itself is therefore 'the very event of obscuring, a descent of the night, an invasion of shadow' (LR 132). In the course of stating this, Levinas claims that the art image leads us into 'a fundamental passivity', that the artist is 'inspired' and that poetic worlds impose themselves on us 'without our assuming them' (LR 132). Obviously intending to present the 'captivation or incantation' (LR 133) of poetry or music as a version of religious participation, these *negative* views of the imaginary or the sensible conflict starkly with the most far-reaching and inspiring moments of Levinas's later ethical postulations. This may explain the excessively dualistic nature of Levinas's moral refusal to engage with the art-work in 'Reality and its Shadow', which the essay itself externalizes onto the artwork by speaking of 'an essential doubling of reality by its image' (LR 136). That is, no reflective admission is permitted of the way in which, on the one hand, art as *mere* image, in Levinas's text, 'does not lead us beyond the given reality' (LR 136), whereas art, considered as image *within* Levinas's text, can lead us somehow precisely to transcend evasion. We might say, indeed, that regarding the artwork as an immobilization of freedom here does to the artwork what the essay claims the artwork itself does to the possibility of criticism. In sum, Levinas gives a highly schematic view in a rather overdetermined essay, and the rigid distinction it insists on, between (good) intellectualism and (bad) idolatry, does not seem to generate good philosophical exegesis any more than it represents good art criticism.

JEAN-PAUL SARTRE (1905–80)

Influential French philosopher who also wrote plays, novels and essays. Leading French figure of *existentialism*, which argued that human beings, unlike objects, create the meaning and essence of their own lives through their existence. The human is therefore *pour soi*, or for-itself, in contrast to the object's state of being *en soi*, or in-itself. Sartre's best-known philosophical works include *L'Imaginaire* (1940), *Being and Nothingness* (1943) and the *Critique of Dialectical Reason* (1960).

THE GRAVEN IMAGE

It is important to bear in mind that this stern mistrust of idolatry and the artwork's 'phantom essence' (LR 137) was also produced by Levinas in an immediate post-war context. As the essay makes plain, he has strongly in mind what he terms the cowardice, evasion and even wickedness of certain artists during the Shoah. Levinas therefore also asserts artistic responsibility here by turning to a traditional Jewish aniconism, or prohibition of images. As we show also in other chapters, this is arguably part of a general return to a specifically Judaic heritage which Levinas undertakes after the war, though he would have repudiated this idea of a return. This fundamental notion of the prohibition of images comes from a prioritizing of the word and from the biblical Second Commandment in Exodus 20: 4 and Deuteronomy 5: 8 which states that 'you shall not make for yourself a graven image'. By the end of the nineteenth century, Western Jewish society could be said to have relocated this explicit commandment in a Protestant culture of the censuring of images, as part of their assimilation. Intellectual evidence of this could be traced in Hermann Cohen's Kantianism, and even in the neo-Kantian presentation of Cubism by the twentieth-century Parisian art-dealer Daniel-Henry Kahnweiler. Later, there is a striking modernist version of aniconism in the work of Franz Rosenzweig, to whom Levinas is obviously indebted. Rosenzweig's *The Star of Redemption*, a key text in the renewal of Jewish theological writing in the early twentieth century, contemplates the Star of Redemption as an ultimate place at the border of being, where vision is simultaneous with an all-encompassing 'mysterious-miraculous light of the divine sanctuary in which no man can remain alive' (SR 424). At a much earlier stage of this book's spiritual journey, Rosenzweig acknowledges that neither oral revelation, beginning with Moses, nor what it views as 'structurally sated paganism, beginning with Plato' (SR 245), has been able to confront art (specifically music in this case) without misgivings. However (and this anticipates some of Levinas's key later appreciations), poetry is here viewed as an exception. Indeed, poetry is held to be the most vital art, in part as it is significantly regarded as the most conceptual: 'poetry supplies structure as well as thought, by supplying what is more than both: conceptual thought' (SR 245).

This dual aspect, informed by Jewish tradition, is obliquely acknowledged by Levinas in his clearly exceptional appreciations of the

Jewish visual artists Jean Atlan and Sasha Sosno, on which I have commented elsewhere (SE 81–86). But it also shows up ambiguously in Levinas's philosophical texts. So, in the 1947 *Existence and Existents*, with its focus on the existential experiences of fatigue, insomnia, the instant and the hypostatic, alongside the notion of the 'there is', art is included as an instance of the latter experience; and the book specifically evokes Cubism in relation to both our apprehension of reality and an occlusion of order. So here we have an iconoclasm where representation is *positively* (that is to say, in Levinasian terms, ethically) obliterated by materialization. Levinas states that through deformation, a painting gives forms, or rather their rationality and luminosity, an absolute existence (the French phrase, *le tableau accomplit l'en-soi même de leur existence*, makes a reference to Sartrean language more obvious). But he then goes on to say that this absolute existence derives in fact from a painter's metaphysical *struggle* with sight itself. So in relation to aniconism, Levinas ultimately reinforces here his contemporary view, given in 'Reality and its Shadow', that art itself does not belong to the order of revelation (LR 132), and that transcendence must fundamentally involve exegesis rather than the image.

FRANZ ROSENZWEIG (1886–1929)

German Jewish philosopher, student of Hermann Cohen and critic of Hegelian philosophy. Following a near conversion to Christianity, Rosenzweig drew on his renewed Jewish faith in order to celebrate in a revelatory manner the relationship between God and humanity, in his major work *The Star of Redemption*.

HEIDEGGER AND DISCLOSURE

We must recognize, finally, that it is not only from these inherited visions, but also from a more obsessive *unsaying* of Heidegger's vision of the artwork, that Levinas's complex and even perturbed view of the artwork is formed. This last influence certainly helps to explain some of the more opaque comments in Levinas's post-war readings of literature. Heidegger's evocative and visionary 1935 essay, 'The Origin of the Work of Art', had presented the artwork as disclosing *aletheia* (that is, truth as an uncovering). For him, Van Gogh's painting of peasant shoes was therefore the *disclosure* of what peasant shoes are *in truth* (OW 161). And just as 'the silent call of the earth' *vibrates* in these shoes (OW 159), according to Heidegger, so in the same way a Greek temple 'illuminates ... that on which and in which man bases his dwelling' (OW 168), namely, an *earth* which through this act becomes a native ground (OW 168). The artwork, then, makes space for Heidegger (indeed, it liberates 'the free space' (OW 170)) and thus 'sets up a world' or 'set[s] forth the earth' (OW 173). From this 'unconcealment' emerges *truth* (OW 176), and as beings we 'stand within and stand out within what is cleared in this clearing' (OW 178). In this vision, art is 'a becoming and happening of truth' (OW 196), and all art, when it does this, is in essence poetry (OW 197), a poetry that *founds*, by 'bestowing, grounding, and beginning' (OW 202). Now, as we shall see, Levinas's post-war approach to different artworks is always tenaciously linked to the detailed ethical task of *undoing* this historical and mystical vision, which can never be dissociated in Levinas's understanding from the evidence of Heidegger's collusion with Nazi ideology.

THE OTHER IN PROUST

Levinas's 1947 'The Other in Proust', published in the journal *Deucalion*, where his evocation of the *there is* had earlier appeared, is contemporary with the essay 'Reality and its Shadow'. Typically, the essay is not really a close reading of the Proustian text. Instead, Levinas gives a rapid and confident overview of the work's historical reception which once again carries references to Fascism and the Shoah, as when he refers to readers who, around 1933, 'became attracted to the literature of action, heroism and the soil' (LR 161). We then reach the essential point, which is that, in contrast to the philosopher, a poet's work for Levinas 'harbours an ambiguity', since 'it is concerned not to express but to create the object' (LR 161). He then immediately evokes those dangers of a quasi-religious 'participation', which are for him inherent in this poetic practice (and by implication in the Heideggerian view of a poem's mysterious and uncanny disclosure): reality appears 'by magic', truth and error are no more than 'spells and incantations', the work's 'charm' permits a giddy amoralism to run unfettered by moral law, nothing is straightforward and 'acts are shadowed by unpredictable "counter-acts" ... that reveal unsuspected perspectives and dimensions' (LR 162). This is already familiar to us from 'Reality and its Shadow'. In short, ethics is here in abeyance. Levinas writes that 'magic begins, like a witches' Sabbath, where ethics leaves off' (LR 162). The image recalls Shakespeare's *Macbeth*, which was itself a key textual reference in *Existence and Existents*, at the point where Levinas had discussed the horror of the experience of the *there is*, and contrasted this to the Heideggerian analysis of anxiety (EE 61–63). Though ostensibly discussing Proust, then, Levinas is again recalling the Heideggerian *aletheia* and 'grounding' when he evokes both 'the way Proust's poetry throws light on a subject' (LR 162) – the original French phrase, 'l'éclairage même de la poésie proustienne', making the link to the Heideggerian *Lichtung* more immediately obvious – and the way this landscape has a moral indetermination even though it may be 'historically and geographically precise' (LR 162).

But giddy suspension is in fact exactly what Levinas wants to exploit at this point, in order to move us away from a hypnotized adherence to the 'interiorization of the Proustian world' (LR 162). Levinas starts to re-cast uncertainty and equivocation ethically, as signalling the moment when a fundamental 'mystery of the other' intrudes into our closed world (LR 163). Beyond any drama of psychological insight, then, Levinas views the absence of Proust's character Albertine as embodying an ethical relation with the Other as absence and mystery. In this way, Levinas can read the work as one that is re-situating philosophy's being in a non-totalizing relation, and then contrast this fundamentally with Heideggerian dis-closure. He therefore concludes pointedly that:

> Proust's most profound lesson ... consists in situating reality in a relation with something which for ever remains other, with the Other as absence and mystery, in rediscovering this relation in the very intimacy of the 'I', and in inaugurating a dialectic that breaks definitively with Parmenides.
>
> (LR 165)

The significance of this last remark lies in the way in which it recalls both the Ancient Greek philosopher of the unity of being, Parmenides, and Heidegger's University of Freiburg lecture of 1942–43 on the subject of Parmenides. In that lecture, Heidegger had concluded that the essence of truth originates as *aletheia*, that it does so in such a way as to conceal itself forthwith, and that this is *the event* of the history of the 'Occident'. It is clear that Levinas's particular re-reading of Proust here carries within it a profound ethical lesson of rejection and caution, loaded as it must be with the knowledge that, at the precise historical and geographical moment of Europe in 1942–43, what was being disclosed as the event of the history of the 'Occident' was the fully operational Nazi programme of mass assassination. In relation to this politics, Heidegger's early collusion and later silence can only turn his mid-war meditations on Parmenides into the worst form of evasion for Levinas.

It is perhaps not surprising, then, that at this stage of reading Levinas still harbours fundamental doubts regarding the degree to which the artwork can carry any lesson at all, let alone one that brings us an ethical consciousness beyond 'participation'. So if Proust's lesson does consist in situating reality in a relation with something that for ever remains other, the potentiality of this lesson still depends for Levinas on whether we can divest ourselves of images and symbols, rhythm and magic, spells and incantations (LR 161). But we have to add that such a potentiality will also seem to depend on whether Levinas is going to overcome a fundamental suspicion which he still appears to harbour at this stage about the artwork in general.

TRANSCENDING WORDS

These complex thematics return two years later in Levinas's essay 'The Transcendence of Words'. This reaction to Michel Leiris's recently published autobiographical volume *Biffures* again moves quickly through a situating and an appreciation of the work, in order to reach that crucial moment where Levinas detects that the artwork 'turns into something other than itself' (LR 146) through an inherent ambiguity. Through Leiris's exploration of how technically and existentially, bifurcation and erasure are inherent in thought, Levinas sees confirmed 'the presence of one idea *in* another' (LR 146) and through this a transcendence of the 'classical categories of representation and identity' (LR 146). The non-visual potential of this overflowing again produces clear references to both Heidegger and the *there is*. Levinas comments firstly that 'the proliferation of erasures is like the return of consciousness to its perceptible existence, and the return of the perceptible to its aesthetic existence' (LR 147). He then adds that this 'can be explained by the very nature of visual experience to which Western civilization ultimately reduces all spiritual life' (LR 147), before concluding that such a civilization 'culminates in an unveiling [*elle aboutit au dévoilé*] and in the phenomenon. Everything is imma-nent to it' (LR 147). It starts to become clear that the rending and overflowing qualities inherent in Leiris's *biffures,* about which we have heard very little in themselves, have the positive value for Levinas of breaking open the 'self-complete world of vision and art' (LR 147), and of permitting the presence of the Other to intrude into a self-sufficient world. Somewhat appropriating Leiris for a rather differ-ent critical purpose, Levinas concludes strongly that Leiris shows how

[t]he subject who speaks does not situate the world in relation to himself, nor situate himself purely and simply at the heart of his own spectacle, like an artist. Instead he is situated in relation to the Other. This privilege of the Other ceases to be incomprehensible once we admit that the first fact of existence is neither being in-itself nor being for-itself but being *for the other*; in other words that human existence is a creature. By offering a word, the subject putting himself forward lays himself open and, in a sense, prays.

(LR 149)

Appreciating the self-opening and self-distancing effects of Leiris's complex involutions, Levinas is able here to approve of an artwork, by reading it as manifesting an ethics of adherence to the other's voice which is inherent in consciousness. But, in spite of the significant mention of prayer at the end of the article, there is still little devel-opment here of a correspondingly responsive transformation of Levinas's ethics which could result more generally from encountering the strange other of the artwork.

MAURICE BLANCHOT

It is with a prolonged involvement with the work of Maurice Blanchot, however, that we finally begin to see how invocation of the artwork itself enacts an opening up to the Other. Several key essays come into play here, spanning twenty years from the mid 1950s on. In them we can see Levinas acknowledge and in turn offer profound new propo-sitions, as he contributes to an intellectual relationship that pushes beyond the separation of philosophy from the artwork. The earliest of the essays on Blanchot, the 1956 'The Poet's Vision', reacts to the publication of Blanchot's *The Space of Literature* the previous year. The crucial lesson which Blanchot might hold for Levinas is indicated in his opening remark that Blanchot's book 'is, in fact, situated beyond all critique and all exegesis' (PN 127), and therefore it can exist generically and inspirationally beyond a rigid demarcation between the artwork and the ethical consciousness. Having (ironically) credited Blanchot and others (including those who want to 'go back to the "truth of being" with Heidegger' (PN 127)) with bringing us to the end of philosophy, Levinas quickly distances Blanchot from remaining with 'being as the measure of all things' (PN 128), given the way in which, through poetic language, he perceives the *there is*: 'the incessant, the interminable', 'the rustle of being' (PN 132), 'the second night', 'lapping, murmur, dull repetition' (PN 133). So transcendence and revelation can here be effected through the voicing of literature, or what literature can lead us to and beyond. Indeed, Levinas is brought to recognize through Blanchot how 'a prior transcendence (though he does not use this term) is required in order for things to be able to be perceived as images, and language as poetry' (PN 130). A remarkable inversion has taken place here, for Levinas is now saying that the transcendent vision in the artwork *precedes* rather than *precludes* the transcendence that comes when philosophy surpasses the image. Indeed, Levinas further specifies that the mode of revelation of what remains other 'is not the thought, but the language, of the poem' (PN 130). In other words, we are not here even talking about just recuperating from the poem whatever enables us to break away from its hypnotizing essence. Blanchot's re-situating of the work of art *outside of* the realm of the Day, which Levinas takes to mean a Heideggerian lighting, so that the work is 'an invitation to leave the Heideggerian world' (PN 135) leads Levinas to an astonishing revision of literature as a fundamental *non-truth*. That is to say, this kind of writing can give a *non*-Heideggerian truth of being (and a *non*-Hegelian negativity as well). It is a *non-true* that is 'the essential form of [non-Heideggerian] authenticity' (PN 135). Thereafter, in pointing up a superficial proximity to Heidegger, Levinas effectively calls out to Blanchot (and to the artwork) to carry on, and so to carry him on, further into a writerly *nomadism*, in the hope that one can move intellectually and poetically away from the Heideggerian illuminated *place* of authenticity and towards the ethical authenticity of dark and rootless exile. Levinas concludes with a new appreciation that is of fundamental significance to his own ethical mission: 'Does not the poet, before the "eternal streaming of the outside", hear the voices that call away from the Heideggerian world?' (PN 139).

This fundamentally new calling to the artwork is powerfully sustained from here on by Blanchot's intellectual companionship. Ten years later, responding to invocations by Blanchot himself in his *Waiting Forgetting*, and following the publication of *Totality and Infinity*, Levinas's 1966 'The Servant and her Master' repeats by now familiar precepts about what exists outside and beneath thought and language, before asserting the worth of the inexpressible and the impossible which Blanchot's art confronts beyond philosophy's limits, and, through this, the worth of poetry itself. Levinas is now able to revise radically the artwork's ethical status by asking: 'is it possible to get out of this circle otherwise than by expressing the impossibility of getting out of it, by speaking the inexpressible? Is not poetry, of itself, the Exit?' (LR 152). So poetry, of itself, is now an *otherwise*, and not 'the philosophical language of interpretation' (LR 153). This comes long before the 1974 publication of *Otherwise than Being*. Poetry now looks to be suggesting and guiding Levinas's most radical philosophical revisions. Through Blanchot's work and readings, Levinas is now prepared, with only occasionally residual hesitations, to acknowledge how poetic language is able to generate signs beyond meaning, abandon the order present to vision and hold open transcendence. As a result, the poem is no longer viewed as an aesthetic object by Levinas. Instead, he significantly aligns it to prayer and prophecy. He therefore concludes in a final footnote:

> [w]e said earlier that the word poetry referred to the disruption of immanence to which language is condemned in becoming its own prisoner. There is no question of considering this disruption as a purely aesthetic event. But the word poetry does not after all name a species whose genus is referred to by the word art. Inseparable from speech, it overflows with prophetic meanings.
>
> (LR 159)

PAUL CELAN

It is perhaps in their respective approaches to the poetry of Paul Celan (a contemporary Romanian-born Jew who wrote in German) that Blanchot and Levinas can also be seen to speak profoundly to each other, no doubt in part because of Celan's complex linguistic witnessing of the Shoah and, indeed, the notorious failed encounter between Celan and Heidegger that is reflected in Celan's poem 'Todtnauberg'. Nonetheless, Levinas's appreciation of Celan's poetry finally carries with it an emphatic and generally unretractable shift in attitude, away from the basic belief that it is prose and not poetry that remains the only appropriate means of communication in the ethical relation. Blanchot's explicit engagements with Celan had included the 1980 *The Writing of the Disaster* which, while powerfully inflected with Levinasian formulations, if anything challenges some of Levinas's own restrictions. In a section leading up to yet another contestation of Heideggerian *aletheia*, Blanchot expounds on Celan's definition of poetry as *cette parole d'infini* ('an expression of infinitude' (WOD 90)). This is Blanchot's translation of a well-known term coined by Celan in a 1960 speech referred to as *The Meridian*, where he describes or at least *speaks of* poetry and its other as 'diese Unendlichsprechung'. Four years later, Blanchot produces *The Last One to Speak*. Here, in addition to using themes that 'The Poet's Vision' had offered him, Blanchot employs an interrupted style of revelatory reading that seems to elaborate in itself a Levinasian ethics of literature. This occurs in response to the obsessive yet attentive voice of Celan's poetry, which we are told offers *witness without witness*. Prior to this, Levinas's own 1972 essay 'Paul Celan: From Being to the Other' had raised both these aspects. Celan's language is here viewed as bearing only superficial similarities to Heidegger's own linguistic effects. It also provokes notions of proximity and responsibility which will recur as integral concepts in *Otherwise than Being*, published two years later. Quoting the above Celan phrase again, but using the French version of it suggested by the poet du Bouchet, Levinas is now in turn prepared to recognize poetry as being a 'conversion into the infinite' (PN 42). Levinas then characterizes this further as being the attempt to *think* transcendence (PN 42), 'the defection of all dimension' (PN 46), and '[m]ore and less than being' (PN 46). Thus described, Celan's poetry already *is* the radical attempt of Levinas's whole *Otherwise than Being*. We have by now reached the opposite pole from the moralizing certainties of 'Reality and its Shadow'. As though astonished by his own transformation, Levinas asks himself in a footnote: 'Transcendence through poetry – is this serious?' (PN 175), but then reacts to his question affirmatively. Far from opposing exegesis to the artwork,

Levinas now sees the latter as providing the model for the former's most radical shifts, and effectively guiding his own forthcoming philosophical work. He specifically asks: 'Does he not suggest poetry itself as an unheard-of modality of the *otherwise than being*?' (PN 46). As an interrogation of, and a seeking for, the Other, poetry and philosophy can now be viewed as sharing the same unrealizable ideal. The rest of the essay therefore draws no categorical or ethical distinctions, associating Celan's work with a 'saying without a said' (PN 43), 'extreme receptivity, but extreme donation' (PN 43), the 'insomnia that is conscience' (PN 43) and 'a signification older than ontology' (PN 46), all phrases that go to the heart of the work of *Otherwise than Being*. In short, the work of Celan now fundamentally *is* the work of Levinas. Pointedly, Celan's poetry also presents to Levinas an unrooted, stateless and utopian world that contests the Heideggerian landscape, and simultaneously evokes a promised land in which one dwells *ethically*:

> this unusual outside is not another landscape. Beyond the mere strangeness of art and the openness of beings on being, the poem takes yet another step: strangeness is the stranger, the neighbour. Nothing is more strange or foreign than the other man, and it is in the light of utopia that man shows himself. Outside all enrootedness and all dwelling: statelessness as authenticity!
>
> (PN 44)

FRIEDRICH HÖLDERLIN

It is clear from the context, finally, that Levinas's full investment in the poetry of Celan is also designed to act as a counterweight to Heidegger's invocation of poetry. This is most obviously true of Heidegger's appreciation of the German lyric poet Hölderlin (1770–1843), including in posthumously published lectures which 'probably contain all Heidegger's "political" thinking' (HAP 134). In the interview collected in *Ethics and Infinity*, Levinas had sought to distinguish the significance of *Being and Time* from the later 'disappearance ... of phenomenology properly speaking [and] the first place that the exegesis of Hölderlin's poetry and the etymologies began to occupy in his analysis' (EI 42). Here as well as in other places, Levinas is looking to establish an unambiguous break between the end of the twenties (and *its* break with a certain humanism, which Levinas had participated in) and the early thirties, most obviously from the moment of Heidegger's rectorate. Heidegger himself engages in a version of this revisionism in his *An Introduction to Metaphysics*, where he speaks of the contemporary political crisis as a 'decision [that] must be made in terms of new spiritual energies unfolding historically from out of the centre' (IM 38–39). As part of this decision, Heidegger recalls his own *Being and Time* even as he associates Hölderlin with 'open[ing] up the way to the future' (IM 126) and 'know[ing] how to wait, even a whole lifetime' (IM 206). Now, the ability to counter the mythifying national aestheticism which Levinas takes Heidegger to be generating, with 'statelessness as authenticity', enables Levinas to view Celan and thus the artwork as a true, prophetic and ethical witnessing. This becomes even clearer if we look at some of the key transpositions of Hölderlin which occur in Heidegger's lecture. Viewed comparatively, we can see that Levinas looks to establish a deliberate and absolute contrast between Hölderlin's *hymn*, as read by Heidegger, and Celan's prayer, as read by Levinas. In Heidegger's version, Hölderlin's hymn moves outside of metaphysics in its poeticization of a human being's passage through the foreign, and in 'the mystery of the coming to be at home' (HH 55). Levinas's appreciation of Celan, in contrast, emphasizes the poverty, inadequacy and non-radiance of a language, a language that therefore signifies proximity *rather than* mastery, and a being for the other *rather than* a world in being. The historical coursing of the Ister, the river that is the subject of Hölderlin's great poem, is in this regard for Levinas the spiritual opposite of the unresolved expulsion and insomnia of Celan's world. Levinas concludes his essay by emphasizing the difference unequivocally. Celan's 'chant' therefore indicates a 'signification older than ontology and the thought of being' (PN 46), while his absolute poem, received as a 'spiritual act *par excellence*', is specifically 'not a variation on Hölderlin's *dicterisch wohnet der Mensch auf der Erde* [man dwells poetically on the earth]' (PN 46).

THE ETHICS OF THE ARTWORK

It is more clear now that Levinas's engagement with the artwork initially involved both suspicion and appreciation, and that this double reaction was both inherited and consciously adopted. Gradually, though, he began to incorporate and so transform this ambiguity.

Beginning, then, with an excessive and overdetermined criticism of the artwork, Levinas came to appreciate, in particular via the intellectual relationship with Blanchot, how the artwork, epitomized at its purest by Celan's poetry, could itself enact an exemplary break with philosophical closure, by giving voice to the significance and obligations of philosophy's other. Belatedly, Levinas saw how an artwork's ethical being could move beyond notions of visuality, category and even content, in order to achieve a moment which Levinas would recognize as a modality of transcendence.

SUMMARY

Levinas's relation to artworks moves from disapproval to intimate appreciation. Key features of this development are:

- Inherited concepts of the image.
- Heidegger's use of poetry.
- Readings of major French works of literature.
- The writings of Maurice Blanchot.
- The poetry of Paul Celan.

TALMUDIC READINGS

From the end of the fifties until late in his life, Levinas regularly produced a Talmudic reading (twenty-five in all), in the first instance for an annual gathering of a recently established Colloquium, the *Colloque des Intellectuels Juifs de Langue Française*. This new activity was in part an extension of the Talmud class which he initiated at the ENIO, and underpinned by his own studies under the enigmatic Talmud scholar Chouchani. Of these Talmud readings, all but two were subsequently published, largely unaltered though not including the responses made to them at the time. Nine of these formed the 1968 *Quatre Lectures Talmudiques* and the 1977 *Du Sacré au Saint* (collectively published in English as *Nine Talmudic Readings*), and a further nine appeared in either the 1982 *Beyond the Verse* or the 1988 *In the Time of Nations*.

In practical terms, these readings traditionally required Levinas to present a text from the Talmud, which itself would naturally include the often conflicting discussions of several sages regarding the meaning of a passage under examination, and in repeating the text, section by section, to offer in turn his own interpretation, which subsequently could be open to cross-examination. In virtually every case, however, Levinas would additionally renew the core text's significance by referring to contemporary philosophical ideas and historical events, and so encourage the Talmud to question current intellectual schemes. This last factor is important for our view of Levinas's work as a whole. For as knowledgeable companions to the explicitly philosophical works, these Talmudic readings, if read closely rather than noted in passing, can fundamentally change our knowledge of 'Levinas'. This chapter outlines the main intellectual contexts of Levinas's Talmudic readings, reviews their complex relation to the philosophical works, examines their thematic, stylistic and ethical dimensions, and anchors these issues in a number of key essays by Levinas.

THE SIGNIFICANCE OF THE TALMUD

The Talmud or 'Study' is synonymous with Jewish thinking practice. Physically, it is comprised of two collections – the Palestinian Talmud and the later Babylonian Talmud – which bring together centuries of discussion and administration of Jewish law by scholars and lawyers up until the sixth century CE. A key feature is that a Talmud text presents not just a *Mishnah*, or teaching based on repetition and study, but also its accompanying *Gemara* or commentary and supplement. Codified into six main orders or *sedarim*, each of which is further divided into several *Tractates*, and defined as either *Halakhah* (legal issues) or *Aggadah* (ethical and moral dimensions), the Talmud generates a practice of potentially endless reading and questioning that is grounded in forms of presentation and constant re-framing.

In the introduction to his first collection of Talmudic readings, *Quatre Lectures Talmudiques*, published in 1968, Levinas himself gives a detailed historical and generic description of the Talmud, while interestingly laying emphasis on a number of additional features that already suggest a personal insinuation into the tradition, less as ENIO director than as a critic of philosophical totality writing in France in 1968. He specifies how the original sages compiling the *Mishnah* 'most certainly had contact with Greek thought' (NTR 4). He says that *Halakhah* and *Aggadah* often push out of their respective classifications, with the former frequently revealing 'a philosophical extension' (NTR 4) that is potentially opened up by the latter category. And he relates how the Talmudic text in itself represents an 'intellectual struggle [*combat*] and courageous opening' (NTR 4) due, above all, to the way it nurtures 'hypercritical' interrogation and *expects* the reader in turn to assume 'freedom, invention, and boldness' (NTR 5).

Struggle and freedom: we are surely not talking just about an academic task. Levinas is also raising a certain political vision when he speaks of how to 'evoke freedom and non-dogmatism in exegesis today [*de nos jours*]' (NTR 5). This 'today' on one level refers to the daily intellectual situation of a Paris Nanterre professor in 1968, who finds himself at the heart of student-led social and intellectual rebellion that is passionately debating notions of freedom, invention and boldness, but who here is discreetly distancing himself from that politics, to the extent of not mentioning it or making only coded and negative allusions. Freedom 'today' is something else for Levinas here: it is primarily an obligation to respond that is freed from categories and made primary. Levinas goes on to signal the shortcomings of both a historical-philological approach to texts, and a purely formalist or structuralist interpretation, before outlining a task of reading that recognizes but also breaks conventions. His reading approach will seek to *translate* a text's meanings into a modern language, so as to link the Talmud 'to the present and to the present's understanding', that is, to the *actualité* (NTR 6).

This also signals a more than secondary status for the Talmud in Levinas's world. It is not just an extension of the Bible, but is rather 'a second layer of meanings; critical and fully conscious' (NTR 7). He notes, in another significant challenge to hierarchies and genres, how the sages who interpreted and nurtured the Talmud, the *Hakhamim*, themselves referred to Greek philosophers as the *Hakhamim* of Greece. And he then quietly recalls '[w]hat Paul Ricœur says about hermeneutics' (NTR 7). (This is the Ricœur who, in 1968 at Nanterre, tried to maintain a discussion with rebellious students, but was persuaded finally to bring the police onto the campus, and who left afterwards to teach at Chicago.) Levinas associates this evocation of hermeneutics with the Talmud's 'dialectical, argumentative language', and contrasts this negatively with structural analysis. In fact, in a clear reference to the work of the anthropologist Lévi-Strauss in particular and structuralist theory more generally, Levinas specifies that nothing is less like the Talmud than 'the structure of "savage" thought' or its *bricolage*' (NTR 7). (The English translation's rendering here – 'the "pottering around" of primitive thought' – obscures the precise allusions to the work of Lévi-Strauss.) So Levinas here is pointedly 'translating' the Talmud into a Western chronology of ideas in order to characterize its aims, but also to challenge assumed priorities regarding philosophy versus the Talmud, or what constitutes a real critical or intellectual revolution. The Talmud may sit now for Levinas within a conception of modernity that begins with Kant, but in so doing it can also complicate such a historical definition through its continued transmission of 'commentaries overlapping commentaries' (NTR 7). Its existence as both a self-constituting and an endlessly deferring text can challenge notions of primary versus supplementary status, including in terms of a 'Greek' Other. And its thinking processes, no less than its chronologies, are just as sophisticated as either biblical exegesis or the latest intellectual revolution, and offer a living and enduring lesson of ethical inquiry.

Levinas then concludes his introduction by relating the Talmud to other, equally significant, forms of freedom, which are again clearly political. He evokes the Liberation of Paris and France during the Second World War, adding that his own mode of reading the Talmud is common to a movement which arose within French Judaism at that historical moment. He speaks of heritage as involving something more than just land (in a veiled negative reference to Heideggerian concepts of founding). And he refers finally to the foundation of the modern State of Israel, which in being mentioned only now carries with it the intellectual and moral weight already attached to the Talmud. In one of several passages wherein he very carefully brings the significance of the Talmud before Israel, Levinas here stresses that returning to a practice of 'reading in search of problems and truths' (NTR 9), which the Talmud pursues in a respectful but unlimited manner, is just as necessary to Israel as the return to an independent political life. Zionism, Levinas believes, 'is not a will to power' (NTR 9). The Nietzschean echo of this phrase is obviously meant to recall everything from the early essay on the philosophy of Hitlerism through to his judgement of contemporary 'anti-humanist' theories like structuralism. Arguing in conclusion for a discursive link between Israel and the West, which would involve both a dialogue and a definite distinction, Levinas seems to define the Talmud and Israel in the same terms. He reinforces this by focusing on the establishment of the Hebrew University of Jerusalem and its 'most noble essence of Zionism', which he says are aiming to preserve and develop the study of the Talmud in a modern idiom surrounded by modern problems. It is with this (arguably idealistic as opposed to real) vision of politics that Levinas can endorse Zionist establishment and even expansion in a most particular way: the 'translation "into Greek" of the wisdom of the Talmud' is 'the essential task of the University of the Jewish State' (NTR 10), and presumably, therefore, of the State of Israel itself.

TALMUD

From the word for learning. A comprehensive term covering the *Mishnah* and *Gemara*, traditionally based on the oral Law transmitted at Mount Sinai, and composed of laws and their discussion, grouped into *Halakhah* or *Aggadah*. The *Mishnah* is the codification of Jewish law compiled by Judah ha-Nasi c. 200 CE, which contains the oral Law traditionally given to Moses at Sinai. The teachers quoted in the *Mishnah* are called the *Tanaim*. The *Gemara* are the traditions, discussions and rulings of speakers or interpreters who comment on the *Mishnah*. The *Halakhah* are the legal texts or dimensions of Talmudic study, in contrast to the *Aggadah*; the *Halakhah* originally being a legal formula laid down in the oral Law. The *Aggadah* are the ethical and moral texts and dimensions of Talmudic study, in contrast to the *Halakhah*, of which they are some time seen as the refinement.

BCE AND CE

Before Common Era and Common Era (equating to the Christian BC and AD).

EXEGESIS

From the Greek meaning 'to lead out'. Critical interpretation of a text, especially of holy Scriptures. Exegesis can be thought of as a practice of hermeneutics, and typically involves close analysis of significant words in the text, together with an examination of their historical and cultural contexts.

STRUCTURALISM

The term used to describe a predominantly French set of theories developed in the 1950s and 1960s which adopts a self-styled scientific approach to writing and reading. The different exponents, working in criticism, psychoanalysis, anthropology or historical research, all based their demonstrations on the assertion that meaning is derived from the position of a fact or phenomenon within a system or structure. *Post-structuralism* developed out of this research, retaining the ideas relating to position and complexity while criticizing some of structuralism's methods and underlying assumptions.

TALMUD OR PHILOSOPHY

'Jewgreek is greekjew. Extremes meet.' Derrida's closing citation of Joyce's *Ulysses*, in 'Violence and Metaphysics', sought to summarize and problematize the relationship between Hebraic and Greek worlds of wisdom in Levinas. As we have noted, Levinas's evaluation of the Talmud (which Derrida's early essay does not comment on) suggests a simultaneous separation and linkage of philosophies and world-views. But such a suggestion itself assumes a rational rather than mystical approach to religious texts. For Levinas, the ethical relation must involve a rational and articulated route to infinity, not an immediate route of enthusiasm and ecstasy. This is evident anyway from the prolonged attention he pays the Talmud, let alone from how it is given methodological attributes, political resonances and the function of resisting dogmatic assertions. We might say that this is a natural choice for an academic Jew from Kaunas, anyway, but it is all the same still a choice, for although Levinas was exposed in the normal way to Talmud study in his childhood, it was only by his admission late 'and on the fringe [*marge*] of purely philosophical studies' that he came to focus on the Talmud.

This new undertaking by Levinas is therefore designed in part to contextualize and extend the limits of philosophy. Levinas is of course aware of the fundamental differences of reference and approach between philosophy and Talmudic readings, and is understandably wary of how an easy equation between them might be used intellectually to dismiss both. Partly as a result of this, he tended to emphasize that he always distinguished between philosophical and confessional texts, not just in their languages and methods but even in terms of their respective publishing houses, just as he equally veered away from the label 'Jewish philosopher'. Nonetheless, when we read the Talmudic interpretations, we can see very clearly how they often 'translate' Levinas's philosophical concerns and even actual texts. Indeed, we can go further: in the way the Tamudic texts transpose into a more domestic and personable form certain fundamental philosophical concerns with originality of discourse, the emergence of truth, synchrony and representation, and even use the precise vocabulary of the philosophy, the Talmudic readings not only enact ethical saying but also open up again those assumptions which even Levinas's philosophy was making regarding the forms and means of expression to be chosen for a grand message of infinity or being-for-the-other. But most crucially, there is no question here of a simple overturning of categories. A more complex relationship is now being suggested to us. Therefore, while the transition from *Totality and Infinity* to *Otherwise than Being* was logical in its own terms, we can now trace how that transition was also being thematically reflected, staged and sometimes even predicted in Talmudic readings from the same periods. This does not produce a mere reversal of hierarchies that would make the Talmudic readings some sort of post-modern grounding of the philosophy. But it does indicate a dialogue that is textual as well as cultural, and recalls Levinas's view of the Talmud's relation to the Bible as involving 'a different authority' that is 'neither inferior nor superior' (NTR 7). Critical reception of the philosophy has insufficiently credited this relationship between the philosophy and the Talmudic readings, which is one that itself displaces decisive notions of priority, source and supplement with a more suspenseful dynamics.

VOICING THE TALMUD

Some of these above ideas are directly present in the dramatic nature of Talmudic readings themselves. A sacred text is presented at the same time as those voices that interrogate both it and one another. To this is also added a presenter's voice, such as that of Levinas, which questions the entirety of the text, the presenter's own understanding and even the understanding of the addressee. Irresolution is therefore the fundamental dynamic of the Talmud, and generates an ever-growing text. This is then further stretched by additional levels of relation, when he introduces philosophical or political references. A form of multiple voicing quickly becomes the norm, with every articulation repeated and changed by its echoes. In the context, it would be surprising, in fact, if a 'Hebrew' or Talmudic voice were not, then, to be contextualized here by a 'Greek' or philosophical consciousness. We therefore almost expect the references to Plato. But more dramatically, the situations encountered in the texts are also presented as being absolutely contemporary: thus we are told that Jacob is engaged in an existential search for integrity (NTR 48), or that Rab Zera has the job of opposing a Hitler (NTR 87). This performative and inclusive gesture extends even to the occasion of the Colloquium itself, for Levinas's readings are obviously acknowledging the multiple yet supposedly homogeneous nature of his audience, among whom he counts himself: namely, *intellectuels juifs de langue française*, French-speaking Jewish intellectuals, with all the overlapping and even conflictual linguistic, cultural, historical and intellectual sets of adherences and resolutions which this designation involves. Levinas has the task, then, not just of reading the text but also of doing all the voices. As a result, we gain a localized, specific and often more under-standable manifestation of many of his dense and allusive philosophical expressions, concerning the idea of infinity within me, or a passivity more passive than all passivity, or of the rupture of immanence.

Much of this hangs on Levinas's masterly performance of the text, with a notable recourse to pedagogical tools that are sometimes absent from the philosophical works: orality and engagement, humour and irony, sarcasm and pathos, delight and intrigue. There are moments of engaging and almost cheeky wit, that remain even in the printed ver-sion, as when, in 'The Temptation of Temptation', Levinas asks incredulously if the Talmudists had actually not read their Corneille; or when, in 'Promised Land or Permitted Land', he refers to defeatist explorers as 'leftist intellectuals'; or when, in 'As Old as the World?', he describes a heretic looking to dodge laws concerning sexual abstention as probably already a Parisian. These little jokes are actually fundamental elements, since they exemplify the humanism, uni-versalism and even atheism that go to the heart of Levinas's ethical presentation of both philosophy and the Talmud. That is to say, they are part of what he elsewhere calls 'A Religion for Adults' (DF 11–23). This religion is one that supposedly affirms a humanism that does not depend on 'extrahuman factors' (DF 20), a universalism that sees 'Israel' here as not depending on 'any historical, national, local, or racial notion' (DF 22), and an atheism, or not-theism, that does not depend on a mystical dissolving of ethical consciousness in divine rapture or spectacular idolatry.

A RELIGION FOR ADULTS

What Levinas is insisting on in each of his Talmudic readings, then, is that ethical 'optics' which he also introduces in the later *Totality and Infinity*. Some of this relationship between the Talmudic readings and the philosophy is borne out by his essay, 'A Religion for Adults'. This was produced in 1957, in the year of the Colloquium's foundation,

Mao's Great Leap Forward, France's reiterated refusal to grant Algeria independence and a withdrawal by Israel of troops from the Gaza Strip.

The essay gives an early location within the Talmud's 'apparently childish language' (DF 18) of the principles and even terminology underlying the ethical relation which the 1961 *Totality and Infinity* presents as a rupture of the Western philosophical tradition. Beginning with an affirmation of monotheism's common language before a multi-faith gathering in a Moroccan abbey, Levinas characterizes the fate of Jews in the Shoah as 'an experience of total passivity' (DF 12), and the suffering of Israel as something that places it 'at the heart of the religious history of the world' (DF 12). Judaism is therefore a universalism. But Levinas then goes on to stress 'the *particular* routes' (DF 13) through which Jewish monotheism keeps faith alive, and pre-eminently the manner in which the tradition of the Talmud keeps at bay the possession and idolatry that 'offend human freedom' (DF 14) and constitute 'a form of violence' (DF 14). Judaism's promotion of 'intellectual excellence' (DF 15), in Levinas's view, is moreover what brings it for him 'very close to the West, by which I mean philosophy' (DF 15). So both Judaism and philosophy, as defined by Levinas, are grounded in the same ethical relation, teaching the same transcendence and approaching the same consciousness of justice (DF 16). It seems, in other words, that Judaism and philosophy are fundamentally the same.

Based on this, Levinas now starts to express one in terms derived from the other. The biblical commentaries by the eleventh-century French rabbinical scholar known as Rashi apparently illustrate how the existentialist notion of the *pour soi* must begin in commitment to the Other. It is the Talmud that directly shows the 'intermediary space' of the ethical relation. Justice, the third party and proximity are all here key terms of Judaism, and their 'interdependence' and 'comingling' are demonstrated within one verse of the Talmud (DF 19). The central philosophical phrase: 'I see myself *obligated* with respect to the Other; consequently I am infinitely more demanding of myself than of others' (DF 21–22), is explained immediately by reference to a Talmudic text, and the constitution of a just society is related to another (DF 21). Meanwhile, these positive references are being contrasted with negative allusions to Hegel (DF 18, 23) and Heidegger (DF 23). In terms of textual and intellectual significance, then, it is adult religion and more specifically its exemplification in the Talmud that are held up as the other of philosophy, including of Levinas's own subsequent *Totality and Infinity*! Far from having a subordinate or supplementary status, the Talmud's exegetical process is here granted an enlightening significance and status in relation to the philosophical work. It does not necessarily surpass philosophy, but it does not either merely illustrate its complexities.

THE TEMPTATION OF TEMPTATION

'The Temptation of Temptation', read to the Colloquium in 1964, advances this relation further. It is a presentation of the Tractate *Shabbath*, 88a and 88b, given within the Colloquium's theme of the 'temptations' of Judaism, and concerned with parts of the second book of the Bible, Exodus, where it relates to covenant and commandment, knowledge and obedience. It eventually formed the second lesson of the 1968 *Quatre Lectures Talmudiques*.

Asserting in prefatory remarks how Plato's State expanded to accommodate everything, temptation included, and sarcastically characterizing Westerners or Christians as those who 'want to taste everything themselves' (NTR 33), Levinas remarks, in an echo of the by now published *Totality and Infinity*, that '[i]n the whole as a totality, evil is added to good' (NTR 33). The temptation of temptation alluded to in the title is of course knowledge itself, which is not here just the catalyst of sin in the Garden of Eden, but is also more sharply viewed as 'philosophy, in contrast to a wisdom' (NTR 34). The subsequent Talmudic reading is therefore also meant to be a critique of a philosophy that seeks to incorporate and so annihilate 'the other in its otherness' (NTR 35).

The Tractate is then presented as exemplifying '[t]he choice of the Jewish way of being, of the difficult freedom of being Jewish' (NTR 37), which among other things also brings the just published 1963 *Difficult Freedom* into relation with philosophy and the Talmud. Levinas wants us to agree how 'the freedom taught by the Jewish text starts in a non-freedom which, far from being slavery or childhood, is a beyond-freedom' (NTR 40). He stresses how his extraction from the Talmudic text of this strikingly Levinasian notion of otherwise than freedom or beyond freedom is permitted and even encouraged by the Talmud itself, for it contains a 'permanent dissonance between what

[it] draws from the biblical text and what is found in that text literally'
(NTR 39). When the Talmud shows a sage rubbing his foot so hard
that blood spurts out, Levinas claims genially that we are being told to
rub the text hard, that is, to push interpretation further, for we are
enjoined always to 'look further' (NTR 42) or to see more (NTR 44).
Talmudic reading is also once again a 'direct optics', not least in its
revelation of how 'seeing the other is already an obligation toward
him' (NTR 47).

This already establishes several complex links to his philosophical
concerns. Coming to a conclusion, Levinas now states that he will 'add
a few philosophical considerations' (NTR 48), which turn out to
anticipate – by some four years in publication terms – the radical
language of the article 'Substitution' which was to become the central
chapter of *Otherwise than Being*. Thus he writes that *Temimut*, the
uprightness or integrity shown by Jacob in the biblical text, 'consists
in substituting oneself for others' (NTR 49), that this beyond-freedom
means that freedom is from the beginning 'un-done [*dé-faite*: thus also
defeat, not victory] by suffering', and that this 'condition (or uncon-
dition [*incondition*]) of hostage is an essential modality of freedom'
(NTR 50). In its primary emphasis on suffering subjectivity rather
than the Other, on the figurations of that ethical position, and on the
linguistic wrenching that seeks to both say and unsay, we have an
absolutely clear demonstration here of how the move from *Totality
and Infinity* to *Otherwise than Being* is actually predicted by, and to a
degree predicated on, a Talmudic reading.

DAMAGES DUE TO FIRE

'Damages Due to Fire' is based on the Tractate *Baba Kama*, 60a–b,
which concerns initially the deliberations in Exodus 22 regarding res-
titution. It eventually formed the fifth and final lesson of the 1977 *Du
Sacré au Saint* [*From the Sacred to the Holy*], having been first presented
to the Colloquium in September 1975. The Colloquium's general
theme of war was obviously suggested in part by the events and fall-
out of the 1973 Arab–Israeli war, including the superpower involvement. On this occasion, Levinas's paper was immediately preceded by
a 'philosophical' (in truth largely political) analysis of war by the contemporary philosopher and expert on both Spinoza and the Middle
East, Robert Misrahi, which notably employed notions of reciprocity

and reversibility (C 8). Levinas, in his own presentation, refers politely to Misrahi's analysis of the rationality of war (NTR 182) and his association of Jewish messianism with the ideals of democratic social-ism (NTR 196), and he also makes a passing reference to the influential military historian and theorist Clausewitz, who is a key referent in Misrahi's talk. But Levinas's real field of inquiry and language nonetheless diverge quickly and fundamentally, as he moves from his Talmudic text's concrete subject, concerning who is responsible if a field catches fire, to consideration of 'what is more war than war' (NTR 182), the pursuit of justice.

Levinas's initial *Gemara* or commentary immediately contains several strikingly 'Levinasian' phrases familiar to us from the philosophy: 'we are responsible also for all the rest, that is what we are meant to understand' (NTR 179); '[c]alamity comes upon the world only because there are wicked persons in the world, but it always begins with the righteous' (NTR 179); '[a]s soon as freedom is given to the angel of extermination, he no longer distinguishes between the just and the unjust' (NTR 179). Here his Talmudic voicing becomes almost a philosophical ventriloquism, in a manner that belies any sup-posed naivety on the part of the Talmud text. Furthermore, the commentary that houses these phrases also includes five *baraitot*, a term which, as Levinas takes care to point out, means 'external' or 'outside' and indicates the introduction of traditions and techniques not included in the *Mishnah* or core teaching.

Finally, in a separate section entitled 'Structure of the Text', Levinas notes how his extract is interesting for the way in which it is actually a legalistic text or *Halakhah* that becomes 'transfigured' into a text concerned with ethics, or *Aggadah*. He then adds that this is how

> philosophical views, that is to say, the properly religious thought of Israel, appear in Talmudic thought. (I do not regret having brought together philoso-phy and religion in my preceding sentence. Philosophy, for me, derives [*dérive*] from religion. It is called into being by a religion adrift [*en dérive*], and probably religion is always adrift.) And this aggadic interpretation of a Halakhah con-cerning fire will end with a new Halakhic teaching: the text thus goes from Halakhah to Aggadah, and from Aggadah to Halakhah. That is its original structure, very remarkable in its stylistic rhythm, but not indifferent to the question preoccupying us. So much for preliminary remarks.
>
> (NTR 182)

What we get here, and in the preceding moments, is a suddenly complex hermeneutic where it becomes impossible to maintain distinctions between discourses in terms of originality, authority or acceptability. Levinas first suggests that properly religious thought emerges through cross-generic transfiguration, then he parenthetically raises the conjunction of philosophy and religion, and then immediately states that philosophy derives from religion *and* that religion itself is already and always in derivation or adrift. And this, we are then told, is original structure, only for all of *this* to be then defined and almost dismissed as being merely preliminary remarks!

Hereafter Levinas proceeds, at times as though his own thinking was adrift, through the text's five moments of *baraita*, or external teachings, picking up along the way insights which often sound familiar to us from *Otherwise than Being*, published the previous year. For example, in tracing the etymology of *Rakhmana* or 'Merciful' back to the word for uterus, Levinas sees that 'God as merciful is God defined by maternity' (NTR 183). A composite bountiful figure then seems to suggest for him the text's own gestation beyond legal questions of liability into an ethical recognition of unending and unsatisfied responsibilities. He then emphasizes again how a rationalist dichotomy of war and peace is ultimately inadequate, describing the fire of the text as a more metaphorical sense of 'total disorder, of sheer Element, no longer in the service of any thought, beyond war' (NTR 187). This phrase surely recalls Levinas's 1934 essay on the philosophy of Hitlerism, which was described there as being 'an awakening of elementary feelings' (RPH 64). And indeed, Levinas next observes that a rationalist epistemology cannot explain Auschwitz, partly as its 'anthropology' and 'perseverance in being' (NTR 188) generate a 'private righteousness' that allow evil to happen by not accepting responsibility. The transformation of the fire into the Element also brings Levinas to suggest that when the text evokes the need to take refuge from an epidemic, it is conjuring up the space or rather a 'no-exit' [*sans-issue*], 'no-place' [*sans-lieu*], 'non-place' [*non-lieu*] of Israel itself. In other words, Israel is here a non-localizable space that exists in response to non-localizable fear. It is in fact a moral and universal space of suffering, and thus '[a]ll men are of Israel' (NTR 191). This mention of 'non-place' recalls also Levinas's description of subjectivity itself near the beginning of *Otherwise than Being*. The next *baraita* then shifts the image of fire again, this time from epidemic to famine. Levinas interprets this as indicating a situation where one precisely has to leave home rather than seek refuge in it, in other words an encoding of a further fate suffered by Israelis down the centuries, namely diaspora and exile. The third *baraita*, which introduces where one should walk to avoid the angel of death, brings Levinas into the more involved thought that there is ultimately no radical difference between war and peace, or even peace and Auschwitz, since murder and evil, even if in the form of social injustice and exploitation, are always present. His response now, in terms again reminiscent of the philosophy, involves recognizing how the text is presenting him with 'a call to man's infinite responsibility' (NTR 193). He finally considers more briefly the fourth and fifth instances of *baraita*, before observing in closing how the text itself reconciles the bringing-together of *Halakhah* and *Aggadah* in its figure of a blacksmith-rabbi, who determines that damage caused by fire is indeed comparable to that caused by an arrow. Levinas reads this as confirmation that war (or fire damage) has a destructive aim (like an arrow), and that 'war criminals do exist!' (NTR 196). But he also homes in more movingly on the final *Aggadah* offered by the text, where reference to the biblical image in Zechariah of a protective wall of fire to be built around Jerusalem seems to hold out promise of reconstruction and transfiguration through the very means of destruction (NTR 196). This is a 'peaceful handling of fire' (NTR 196), which could derive, of course, from the use of sacred texts themselves (since the Torah is sometimes traditionally described as having letters of black fire in a frame of white fire). In this mature example of his Talmudic readings, then, we can see how Levinas emphasizes how the Talmud's endless practice of 'reading in search of problems and truths' gradually reveals a universal significance that in no way comes secondary to the sensitivities of a phenomenological analysis, and even predicts and guides the most radical formulations and re-orientations of Levinas's own philosophy.

SUMMARY

Levinas's Talmudic readings develop a relationship both within themselves and to the philosophical works that cannot be thought of as secondary or supplementary. Key features of this development are:

- The significance of the Talmud to Judaism and to Levinas as a scholar.
- The significance of the Talmud to Levinas's philosophical conceptions and practices.
- Levinas's readings of major lessons from the Talmud, and the techniques which the practice develops.
- The Talmud readings 'The Temptation of Temptation' and 'Damages Due to Fire'.

7

POLITICS

Politics lies at the heart of all Levinas's work, whether as the traumatic background or as the changing context of his intellectual development. But it is often viewed as what his work is *not*, namely the failure to achieve a transcending ethics. Yet as the revelation of infinity in the ethical relation is unavoidably human in Levinas, and as the position of a third party becomes essential to his ethical presentation of justice, so there is actually an inherent relation in Levinas between the ethical and the political. But this is still a view that implicitly regards the political as a passage towards ethics which inevitably involves compromise. This slightly stiff and even unreal dichotomy sometimes produces an unstable dynamic of human guilt and bleakness versus messianic hope, or absolute assertion versus absolute scepticism. This is partly the case since the universality that Levinas's writings look to retrieve or prophesy can depend paradoxically on pointing out political and metaphysical shortcomings in a rather apocalyptic tone, rather than noting an altogether more banal politics that just needs to be negotiated. This chapter traces the development of some of Levinas's most interesting and often overlooked post-war writings against key elements of their political background. In so doing, it spells out the implications for the political of the Levinasian ethical, but it also focuses on key texts by Levinas which at certain remarkable points demonstrate that there are political limitations even within Levinas's aspirations.

FREEDOM AND COMMAND

In 1953, the American aid to post-war Europe known as the Marshall Plan had come to an official end, Stalin died and Yugoslavia adopted a constitution. In parallel to these changes, Levinas's contemporary essay 'Freedom and Command' can be read as an important step in a post-war reconstruction of his own ideas. As part of its own philosophical and political re-founding, this rather muscular essay returns logically to its own first principles, as well as referring obliquely to its immediate political context, by focusing on Plato's *Republic*. This becomes a touchstone text that enables Levinas to review and to criticize key terms from Hegel, Husserl and Heidegger as located now in a political context. Importantly, the solitary and denuded hope expressed at the end of *Existence and Existents* has strengthened here into a rather determined view of the State's necessity, one which is pursued with a tough attitude that contrasts with the agonized unknowing of the earlier text. Connections to *Existence and Existents* are still made from the opening, by differentiating the person who labours from the one 'who orders others to labour and to war' (CP 15). This leads Levinas to present the relationship between freedom on the one hand, and a command on the other hand, in a clear and unforgiving manner. If freedom can involve refusing to undergo an action, he writes, then giving a command can only involve already agreeing with the will that is being commanded. So the command is not simply external to the will. We are inevitably reminded of Levinas's survival in the labour camp, and of the work of those who acted as guards and overseers. But, equally, Levinas can therefore also view the notion of freedom of thought as being in itself a form of internal tyranny. Levinas rhetorically reminds Plato at this point that whereas Socrates 'has a fine death', by being able to dominate intellectually his unjust death sentence, we (in 1953) now know that 'the possibilities of tyranny are much more extensive' (CP 16), and extend to the extermination of 'even the ability to obey on command' (CP 16). Though totalitarianism and the death camps are not mentioned, we can clearly hear a reference to them in Levinas's statement that the 'very refutation of human freedom' through complete servility is 'the most painful experience of modern man' (CP 16). He adds, indeed, that a tyrant's power can be so total that there will be no other bent to the tyrant's will, merely 'material exposed to violence'; and the tyrant is therefore in reality alone (CP17). But what does remain free is the ability to foresee this situation and to insure against it. It is this idea, which has been arrived at in a sometimes rather coded way, that Levinas uses in order to assert the necessity of the State: '[f]reedom, in its fear of tyranny, leads to institutions, to a commitment of freedom in the very name of freedom, to a State' (CP 17). There is, then, a way in which freedom involves obedience to law, by 'setting up a world' that defends against tyranny. In this way, we command ourselves, as 'the political condition for freedom' (CP 17).

Here, though, into the setting-up of a world, Levinas needs to reintroduce ethics, since it is obvious even that over time institutions can and will degenerate into a mere adherence to order 'in which freedom no longer recognizes itself' (CP 17). Levinas's guarantee against this comes down to persuasion, speech and a face-to-face situation. He relates the 'idea of a discourse before discourse, of a relationship between particulars prior to the institution of rational law' (CP 18) back to Plato (rather than NATO, we might say), and then pointedly disassociates this kind of face-to-face scenario from either a Heideggerian dynamic of dissimulation and disclosure or some sort of abstract Husserlian rationality. It is tempting to conclude that Levinas's vision here resembles a kind of Russian doll, where freedom is enclosed by politics which is then enclosed by ethics. Certainly, Levinas rejects a political view of politics, and – in a foretelling of Cold War politics – views competing freedoms as a dynamic that can culminate in war (CP 22). The rational order that Levinas appeals to, in the end, is effectively philosophy, presented contentiously perhaps as 'the divine wisdom dwelling within us' (CP 23). By the end of the essay, then, we are supposed to have reached the opposite of our starting point, since for Levinas written law requires discourse which requires encounter, which involves being able to command the self by virtue of the other's command. But this conclusion has also tightly circumscribed how 'freedom', viewed in a post-war political climate, may be considered, how it may find its own limits, what its prior responsibilities are, and how this may be argued and defended.

COLD WAR

We can see that, although this is nowhere acknowledged in 'Freedom and Command', some of Levinas's attitude and even conclusions derive from the large political developments of the day, which saw the formal creation of both NATO and the Warsaw Pact. Certain occasional essays of the period, however, acknowledge this context. The 1956 'On the Spirit of Geneva' comments on the recent Geneva Conference during which the victors of the Second World War agreed, for the first time, to meet to discuss disarmament and the improvement of East–West relations. Interestingly, it takes an almost Heideggerian view regarding atomic weapons development, as well as searching in vain for a true face-to-face situation in post-war 'cosmo-politics' wherein 'men are smiling at one another … without deception but with mistrust' (UH 103). Continuing with the theme, the 1960 'Principles and Faces' scorns a propagandistic speech by the then Soviet leader, Khrushchev, while nonetheless repeating the same desire to see 'impersonal Reason' surpassed and governed by the person-to-person relationship (UH 106). In both articles, we can see that Levinas's supra-political position is consistent with the tough view expounded in 'Freedom and Command' regarding how Western politics must transcend the competition of freedoms.

This background perhaps helps to explain the intemperate nature of a minor piece like 'The Russo-Chinese Debate and Dialectics', printed in the anti-communist journal *Esprit* in 1960. Expressing irritation with the 'scholastic dialectics' (UH 107) of international disputes, Levinas here displays open hostility towards Chinese communism (which was at that point dangerously angry with Khrushchev over his unwillingness to give Mao nuclear weapons). Part of Levinas's anger obviously stems from his stated belief that Chinese nationalism resembles National Socialism and should not be appeased. In keeping with the earlier logic, we are therefore told bluntly to recognize the political truth and be prepared to deal with it: 'we should have been a bit Chinese and start calling a spade a spade again [*pour appeler à nouveau un chat un chat*] and recognize in nationalistic anticapitalism the shadow of National Socialism' (UH 109). But Levinas's coarse stereotyping and brute opposition here seem to break out of his own containment of competing freedoms. The piece's imposed reason reaches its aggressive height when Levinas writes:

In abandoning the West, is Russia not afraid of drowning in an Asian civilization that will, in the same way, subsist behind the apparent concrete of the dialectical conclusion? The yellow peril! It is not racial but spiritual. Not about inferior values but about a radical strangeness, strange to all the density of its past, where no voice with a familiar inflection comes through: a lunar, a Martian past.

(UH 108)

It is a rather ugly moment, in which Levinas seems to betray not just his own experience of being cast as foreign, but also his own most radical postulations. The overdetermined political goal that leads him to appeal to a 'Russia' that has 'belonged' to European history 'for almost a thousand years' (UH 108) could perhaps also be understood as the personal cultural identification of a European intellectual whose childhood language was mostly Russian, but it is still a crude political particularism that contradicts Levinas's own philosophical under-standing.

Nor is it unique. In the 1961 article 'Jewish Thought Today', first published in the Jewish review *Arche*, before being collected in the first edition of the 1963 *Difficult Freedom*, where it is in fact the essay that opens the section called 'Openings', Levinas gives a quasi-historical review of the evolution of Judaism in Europe from its dealings with Christianity up to the present and its Zionist 'dawning of the new world' (DF 166). At this historical point, the new State of Israel is viewed as having given Jewish universalism a 'new-found authenticity' (DF 165), by permitting it for the first time to gauge its task only by its own teachings. Into this scenario, Levinas then introduces the spectre of a new threat, that of materialism. However, he chooses to locate this materialist threat in 'the rise of the countless masses of Asiatic and under-developed peoples' (DF 165), that is in a faceless plurality that is significantly made up of 'peoples and civilizations who no longer refer to our Sacred History, for whom Abraham, Isaac and Jacob no longer mean anything' (DF 165). Recognizing in these masses' voices 'the cry of a frustrated humanity' and a 'hunger of others', Levinas nonetheless seems to de-face these others by desig-nating them in a non-differentiating, non-analysed and plural way, as being 'countless', 'hordes', 'different', 'enormous', a 'vastness', 'foreign' and 'impenetrable'. In a contradiction of some of his own most moving writing, he also seems to de-face an ethical encounter with them by regarding their atomized presence as the persistence of a basic need: they thus remain the cry, the hunger, 'the greedy eyes', the 'hope', the 'gaze'. This dehumanizing characterization is done ultimately to encourage a Judaeo-Christian alliance built around a common legacy of monotheism, so that a new 'fraternity' and the resurgence of a 'forgotten kinship' (DF 165) can take place. Such a characterization of materialism, from a philosopher of the other who survived the consequences of xenophobia, the actions of racial and cultural stereo-typing, the mass exterminations of dishonoured people, and the physical and psychological deprivations of a labour camp, is a painful embarrassment. What is perhaps significant, though, is that such a characterization erupts in the context of a yearning evocation of a messianic hope, which Levinas seeks to locate within the State of Israel.

NATO

The North Atlantic Treaty Organization is an alliance of 26 countries from North America and Europe which came into being via a treaty signed on 4 April 1949, that enjoined democratic nations to safeguard the post-war peace. Largely seen as a capitalist threat by the Soviet Union and its allies, it led to the formation of the so-called *Warsaw Pact*, or Warsaw Treaty, officially known as the Treaty of Friendship, Co-operation and Mutual Assistance, in 1955. This organization of Central and East European communist states sought to counter the alleged threat from the NATO alliance. The existence of these two entities was bound up with a post-war period of hostility that stopped short of full-scale military action called the *Cold War*. This was a protracted geo-political, ideological and economic antagonism between two blocks of nations, and principally the superpowers the United States of America and the Soviet Union, from the end of the Second World War and up to the collapse of the Soviet Union on 25 December 1991 (though effectively by 1985).

NIKITA KHRUSHCHEV (1894–1971)

Leader of the Soviet Union after the death of Joseph Stalin until 1964 when he was removed from power and spent the last seven years of his life under house arrest. His outspoken nature caused occasional diplo-matic embarrassment on the international scene.

MAO ZEDONG (1893–1976)

Chinese Marxist who led revolution and civil war before announcing the establishment of the People's Republic of China in 1949. Maintaining control, until his death, he ushered in mass programmes, such as 'The Great Leap Forward', designed to transform China into a modern industrialized nation. Some of these proved to be disastrous, and are estimated to have led to the possible death of tens of millions.

DIASPORA

The dispersion and settlement of the Jews outside Palestine after their Babylonian captivity. More particularly, in the medieval period Jews in northern and western Europe were often persecuted and then expelled from the countries where they lived. In the twentieth century, many Jews emigrated from Europe to the United States, and many others sought to return to Palestine. The post-war establishment of the State of Israel and the emigration of many Jews to there have more recently affected again the nature of Jewish life in the diaspora.

ZIONISM

From the Hebrew for one of the names of Jerusalem. Zionism in its broadest sense is a term denoting the desire to return to the historical homeland, this being an important theme of diaspora Judaism. In more modern times, the term denotes a nationalist drive which grew from the early twentieth century in response to anti-Semitism and promoted the (re-)colonization of a specific homeland for the Jewish people. Since the eventual foundation of the modern State of Israel in 1948, the term then also came to mean a national ideology within that State, and external support for the State.

DIFFICULT FREEDOM

Levinas's political remarks of the fifties come into sharp focus with the collection of articles all relating to Judaism, published in 1963 (and again in expanded form in 1976) as *Difficult Freedom*. It is in fundamental ways a complex and even overcompensating work. Apart from spanning nearly three decades of rapidly changing world politics in which the new State of Israel (founded in 1948) was often involved, the essays gain further complexity from the interplay of singularity and universalism that Jewish identity faces both individually and exemplarily. Incorporating a re-founded political and ethical being in Levinas's Jewish heritage, reactions to the new State and a delicate dialogue with Zionist ideology, Levinas's texts remain simultaneously attentive and resistant to the political, cultural and even literal mappings of Jewish identity. This tension between support and critique in itself constitutes a further difficult freedom.

On occasions, this ambivalence is resolved through commentary on socio-cultural developments. The 1956 'For a Jewish Humanism' argues simply that the teaching of Hebrew supports a Judaism 'which cannot remain indifferent to the modern world' (DF 273) precisely by enabling Jews to continue to benefit from the Talmudic wisdom that already encapsulates a civilization and teaches a universalist ethics. The 1963 'Means of Identification' externalizes the balancing act, by positing that '[b]etween *already* and *still* Western Judaism walks a tightrope' (DF 50) in its maintenance of an ethical consciousness that interacts with Western contemporary value systems. Elsewhere, as in 'The Diary of Léon Brunschvicg' (1949), the ambivalence is located in a tension between diasporic Judaism and a new muscular State of Israel that is less interested in 'two thousand years of participation in the European world' than in working a land and defending it as 'farmers and soldiers' (DF 39). This relates also to the new State's turning away from a Christian-dominated past that constitutes a profound part of European Jewry's difficult freedom.

Levinas's ambivalence also shows up in certain contrastive gestures. His 1950 'Place and Utopia' recalls how, notwithstanding acts of bravery and integrity, Christian Europe permitted 'the extermination of six million defenceless beings' (DF 99). Rather than emphasize a Judaeo-Christian common heritage, this time Levinas contrasts a Christian desire to transcend human action with a Jewish choice to exist on the level of ethical action. Judaism is inherently historical, existing *in* time, rather than choosing to treat history as a 'test whose goal is the diploma of eternal life' (DF 100). But this Judaism is also pre-eminently that of a diasporic culture, which now also faces disregard by a younger generation of Jews, who are faithful only to notions that are 'foreign' (DF 100–101). In a remark directed as much to the architects of the new Israel as those Christians whose faith 'moves mountains', then, Levinas points out finally that separating God's reign from Caesar's actually reassures Caesar, and thus suggests that the State of Israel is both preceded and superseded by Judaism as a moral living. Contrastingly, the 1951 'The State of Israel and the Religion of Israel' moves in the opposite direction, from initial scepticism to conscious endorsement. It laughs first at the State's trappings, 'a Jewish uniform or a Jewish stamp' (DF 216), and attributes the State's real significance to a religious past that is supplanted by 'modern political life' yet continues to exceed state structures (DF 217). But it then attempts to endorse the State precisely in terms of the living law, since it 'finally offers the opportunity to carry out the social law of Judaism' (DF 218). So the State must exist in order for it to enable its own outstripping by Judaism. Alongside this complex anachronism, Levinas even defers distinctions based on devotion, stating in a moment of total politics that the State of Israel has religion as its *raison d'être*. His joke that such falling away from ritual practice 'happens in the best of families' (DF 219) domesticates the politics and ritualizes the family. The suggestion is that 'the Jewish people', as they here become, themselves constitute religious practice, in the wake of the disappearance of practice as a diasporic fidelity. In a phrase that here seeks to evoke the kibbutz but in other hands could serve a hollow nationalism, Levinas even states that 'if ritual is valuable, it will be reborn only in the virility of action and thought' (DF 219). From then on, Levinas presents study of Scripture as the link between the Jewish religion and what he also explicitly terms 'the Jewish State', but without here being careful enough to specify how study in itself necessarily safeguards against what his own contemporary essay recognized as the potential degeneration of the rational order to the point where freedom one day no longer recognized itself.

The endorsement is made more lyrically, and therefore in argumentative terms more unidimensionally, in an article nonetheless entitled 'Space is not One-dimensional'. This was originally published in *Esprit*, and thus was consciously directed in part at a non-Jewish audience, and in April 1968, which is to say both less than a year after Israel's Six-Day War with the Arab states of Egypt, Jordan, Iraq and Syria, and less than a month before a different, internal eruption in French society commonly referred to as May '68. The article can therefore be incidentally contrasted with a contemporary piece, 'Humanism and An-Archy', which, with the events of May '68 more directly in view, again employs the bizarre image of residence on a lunar landscape (HO 48) by a non-human order which here seemingly comprises anti-humanist promulgators of structuralist anthropology! Fortunately, 'Space is not One-dimensional' is not more of this science fiction. Instead, the title's multidimensionality refers to the article's sincere belief that a French Jew (such as Levinas) can remain totally loyal to France while supporting Israel through the Six-Day War. An apology for the State of Israel therefore firstly involves a recollection of Jewish historical loyalty and devotion to France. The Revolution, the Crémieux Decree (which had granted full French citizenship to Algerian Jews in 1870; it was repealed in 1940 by the collaborationist Vichy regime, and restored in 1943), the Dreyfus Affair and even the Nazi persecution are therefore in part binding elements that rein-forced a Jew's pride in being French and a 'metaphysical' adherence to 'a country that expresses its political existence with a Trinitarian emblem which is moral and philosophical' (DF 261). This bond, however, can then permit a family disagreement (DF 260) over the actions of Israel, which Levinas wishes to see a 'great free nation like France' endorse (DF 260). If a 'new way of being a Jew in France' (DF 259) has come into existence since June 1967, what the article hopes for is in turn evidence of a new France, one that is 'open to the winds of the spirit blowing over the world' (DF 260). This new France will respond to 'a new sensibility within emancipated Judaism' (DF 262), recognize how the 'resurrection of the State of Israel ... can no longer be separated from its doubly religious origins: a Holy Land resuscitated by the State' (DF 264), and will therefore add a fourth dimension, that of religion, to its official national values of liberty, equality and fraternity.

This fantastical image of a total politics establishing itself in a newly religious France leads to an amazing concluding paragraph that effec-tively re-writes French Republican values in the context of Jew, Christian, communist and (for Levinas) even Muslim, in order to evoke a future state that would somehow exist beyond political and national categories and therefore beyond France itself: '[t]o be a fully conscious Jew, a fully conscious Christian, a fully conscious commu-nist, is always to find yourself in an awkward position within Being. And you too, my Muslim friend, my unhated enemy of the Six-Day

War!' (DF 264). The logical and sentimental belatedness of the Muslim's inclusion in this greater religious fraternity, a rhetorical inclusion that surely betokens a residual exclusion, in itself exposes the pretension of an inclusive new state. This ideal space still has a finite number of dimensions, though it has at least shifted the shape of that Platonic state to which Levinas had returned when he was seeking to re-found his ethics in a political context shortly after the end of the war.

ZIONISMS

The difficult freedom that has emerged so far as a fragile alliance of moral and political realities is also tackled in the 1982 *Beyond the Verse*, whose final section is explicitly entitled 'Zionisms'. The 1979 essay 'Politics After!' is typical of the political localization of issues (its immediate context being the historic visit of President Sadat of Egypt to Israel in 1977) and the complex torsions which political realities represent for the ethical identity which Judaism holds for Levinas. It also gathers in many of his key political terms developed over decades. By first praising Sadat for making a bold gesture 'beyond politics' (LR 279), the essay is able to argue that purely political thinking cannot solve the problem of Israel's co-existence with its Arab neighbours, given its insistent dismissal of the human dimension from the order of events: 'the sense [*sens*] of the human, between peoples as between persons, is exhausted neither by the political necessities that hold it bound nor by the sentiments that relax that hold' (LR 278). This reasonable statement then facilitates the suggestion that Israel cannot just be explained or judged politically: presenting the nature of the *one* 'Jewish people' as evidence of the redundancy of political conceptualization, Levinas recalls Israel's 'ethical destiny' and its 'difficult freedom' (LR 279). So Israel's exemplary existence as 'one extreme limit of human potential' arguably disrupts categorizations based on another's smug sovereignty or geographical confidence (LR 279). Evoking a negative kind of universalism which Judaism both owns and 'corrects' by virtue of a global anti-Semitism, Levinas insists that Zionism transcends political doctrine because of its primary focus on the Promised Land (LR 280–81). He then raises and contests the scenarios that are often suggested regarding Israel's military state of being: the power facing the unarmed Palestinian people is actually 'fragile and vulnerable'; this imperialist nature actually 'bears suffering and dereliction deep within itself'; this derivative of Western ideologies is actually haunted by the memory of Massada (LR 282). Israel's 'politics' is described, instead, as a general form of despair. Therefore, the State of Israel is not a state like any other, because it represents 'concrete conditions for political innovation' and it is 'one of the great events of human history'. Instead, it is an embodiment of prophetic morality, and a concept that transcends political thinking (LR 283). This is an astonishingly complex post-political construct that also conflicts uncomfortably with Levinas's previous critiques of forceful assertion. We have an absolute entity that cannot be judged by politics but is justified in part through recourse to the history of politics. A positively presented entity that is singular, vilified and hemmed-in is contrasted with a negatively presented, homogenized and unopposed other, 'rich in natural allies, and surrounded by their lands' (LR 282). The ethical agony of Israel's own politics, on its own land, means that it cannot be judged by others elsewhere. Its difficult freedom seems to involve bearing a uniqueness which the voice of the other therefore can no longer command.

Some of these difficulties are evident also in the oral contortions of an interview given by Levinas on Radio Communauté, on 28 September 1982, which took place in the aftermath of a massacre the previous fortnight, in the Palestinian camps of Sabra and Chatila. Permitted to enter the camps by Israeli Defence Forces, Phalangists murdered several hundred people over a two-day period with no Israeli intervention. In a discussion that was recorded in his house, and perhaps contains an unease that Levinas felt for this kind of technical process, the philosopher spoke of general responsibility 'even if I am not speaking of direct guilt' (LR 290). The philosopher Alain Finkielkraut then boldly raised 'the temptation of innocence', or unaccountability, that Israel arguably gives itself by virtue of its persecuted past. Levinas's reply, while acknowledging the idea, nonetheless evoked the Holocaust and while stressing personal responsibility added that defence also had a place, as 'a politics that's ethically necessary' (LR 292). Finkielkraut then raised precisely the problem of the 'reason of State' which Levinas's 'Freedom and Command' had examined thirty years before, to which Levinas replied by saying that Zionism was still a political idea with an ethical necessity and justification (LR 292), and suggesting that events in Israel were always also a universal arena wherein the relationship between ethics and politics was being played out. At this point Shlomo Malka, the programme's presenter (and later biographer of Levinas), directly put the point that for the Israeli the 'other' here is above all the Palestinian. Levinas's non-committal reply spoke of the other as neighbour, someone who can nonetheless attack another neighbour: '[t]hen alterity takes on another character, in alterity we can find an enemy, or at least then we are faced with the problem of knowing who is right and who is wrong' (LR 294). After an exchange about the potential confusion of mysticism and politics in Israel, Levinas clarified that for him Zionism had a genuine messianic element in its daily determination to lead an ethical life. Finkielkraut added that demonstrations in Israel against the massacres proved also that the values upheld by the Jews of the diaspora were also 'the truth of Israel'. Seizing on the phrase, Levinas stated that the events in the camps showed that Israel had to remain close to its holy books and that this was 'the supreme threat: that our books should be in jeopardy!' (LR 296). He then cited two Talmudic texts concerned with calumny or false representation, one of which Levinas had commented on in his 1965 Talmudic reading 'Promised Land or Permitted Land', whose concern was certainly with the just Zionist but which also recollected at one point one of Israel's contemporary enemies saying that they were 'one hundred million strong to crush you' (NTR 68). It is clear that the spontaneous nature of the format led Levinas to make edgy and cautious remarks. But what also emerges clearly, highlighted perhaps by this same format, is the profound set of difficulties which the State of Israel and Zionism represent for Levinas's ethics *as articulated*, that is to say difficulties that create an unavoidable re-ontologization of the ethical through the projection of an isolated and exemplary political status. An anxiety about this contradiction seems to produce wilful deafness: we hear a reluctant recognition of an other that is hurriedly transposed into a regurgitation of published ethical writing or made equivocal through the re-introduction of ontological and political calculations regarding knowing who is right or wrong. Reference to the supreme threat being the one that is posed to books, moreover, while obviously of ethical import for the guiding principles of Israel in Levinas's view, can also here sound astonishingly naive or even indifferent in the context of real massacres; while appeal to a Talmudic text, albeit one which warns that those who conquer a country 'not only commit themselves to justice but also apply it rigorously to themselves' (NTR 68), seems here complacently academic, and a comprehension of being that Levinas's own mature philosophy exposes so convincingly at the heart of Western philosophy. In the admittedly difficult and compromised freedom of a radio interview, Levinas's reactions seem to fail the test of his own rigorous ethics.

OUR POLITICS AND ETHICS

While politics inevitably involves thematization, Levinas still seeks to postulate a universalist reality that can be somehow pre-political and post-political. This kind of reality would live out an absolute ethics, or an ethics beyond ethics. We have seen how, in Levinas's philosophical, critical and Talmudic readings, this prophetic aspiration employs an ethical saying that tries to act as an unsaying of totalization. Within this resistance to the said, however, we have also seen now how a tenacious unsaid can continue to lurk, and on rare occasions can erupt even within Levinas's language as an instance of persistent political limitations. Such glimpses of intolerance, impatience and reduction of the other, however unguarded and merely inadequate, can unsay any amount of complex unsaying, and not just as a momentary indiscretion but rather as what Levinas himself would call a wound, a trauma or a rending. As we have observed, such a moment, when it occurs within Levinas's work, seems to indicate above all a *merely* political eruption that discredits the work of the ethical. If this can hold for a Levinasian reading of aspects of Heidegger's writing, then it has to hold also for our reading of aspects of Levinas.

In the end, though, there is little purpose in pointing to an occasional political refusal of the other as the chink in Levinas's armour. Far from being just fundamentally damaging, there is even a sense in which these moments of deafness to one's own ethics are the most instructive and even logical. Indeed, it is actually necessary for us here to resist the opportunity to make only politics of politics, if we are to extract the true lesson of ethical vigilance, which is that even a work like 'Levinas' has to remain vigilant, and acquire a certain decolonization. All the more reason, then, why instances of intolerance or 'allergy' in the most sustained de-ontologizing writing of the twentieth century (which of course seem worse for being there) must, if they are to be read ethically, generate not just a counter-political language in us, but also a redoubled consciousness regarding our own critical elaborations.

SUMMARY

Politics influence all of Levinas's writings, and complicate our view of his ethics.

Key features of this aspect of his writing are:

- The post-war considerations of concepts of freedom.
- The articles written during the 'Cold War' period.
- The book *Difficult Freedom*.
- The essays on Zionism.

AFTER LEVINAS

'Generation Levinas?' The question put on 6 January 2006 by the French newspaper *Le Monde* when noting the centennial celebrations of the philosopher's birth was in itself confirmation of Levinas's rapid rise from respected footnote of phenomenology to key representative of a decisive shift in Western philosophy's history. Since his death, the influence of Levinas's writing has spread far beyond the domains of French post-war reflection to influence whole currents of discussion in critical thinking, international relations, aesthetics, spiritual life or psychoanalysis, as well as in 'continental philosophy'. In spite of often profound differences and disagreements, much recent original criticism inspired directly or indirectly by Levinas seems to indicate a real collective desire to understand how notions of ethical being and absolute answerability are significant factors in large and even global moves beyond the old sureties and antagonisms of identity politics.

Inevitably, though, given the rapid expansion of interest in Levinas's work, especially in areas that go beyond Levinas's own knowledge or interests, this has also produced a plethora of 'Levinasian' positions, some of which cite Levinas uncritically in order to refresh a discrete subject with a quick ethical make-over, others of which denounce a frankly unread Levinas in order to re-assert a particular ideological stance. Both types of appropriation contradict Levinas's

own de-thematization of ethical saying. Rather than sedulously catalogue
uses of Levinas and occasionally challenge examples of reductive criticism,
though, it is much more efficient and instructive, surely, to review
some recent examples of the most challenging responses to Levinas.
There are, in fact, a telling number of key contemporary thinkers who
have sought, through close and even interrelated readings, to raise the
implications posed for their world of inquiry by Levinas's ethics, and
have moreover done so in rigorous ways, to the point where we are in
turn properly obliged to re-assess our own provisional understandings
of Levinas. Inevitably, such advanced appreciations of Levinas at a
certain moment move beyond the level of application, in order to raise
the stakes for critical thinking in general. As such, they have in turn
often become key points of reference in continuing debates that concern not just the fidelities, possibilities and shortcomings of Levinas's
work, but also the general conditions and challenges that face intellectual or political or aesthetic discussion today.

WELCOMING LEVINAS: JACQUES DERRIDA

There could be no more fitting place to begin a review of how one
continues to think 'after Levinas' than with his most challenging and
yet most welcoming reader: Jacques Derrida. The 1996 'A Word of
Welcome' forms the main text of Derrida's *Adieu to Emmanuel Levinas*,
which was published in its entirety the following year. In the book
form it is prefaced by the funeral oration, given by Derrida himself for
Levinas on 27 December 1995, the title of which – 'Adieu' – is
obviously reflected in that of the book, and whose mode of direct
address returns at the end of 'A Word of Welcome'. This latter text
transcribes Derrida's opening lecture in the 'Homage to Emmanuel
Levinas' conference marking the first anniversary of the philosopher's
death. At first reading, we are perhaps struck and even frustrated by
Derrida's recourse to discretion, suspension or retention: we are constantly told that he feels guided by a question that he will 'in the end
leave in suspense' (AEL 19); that '[w]e cannot take up these questions
here' (AEL 39); that he has already raised a question 'in a text to
which I do not wish to return here' (AEL 43); that another issue is
something he 'might speak about later' (AEL 44); that another
thought 'might be the place for a future meditation' (AEL 97); and
even that '[t]hese questions are not posed' (AEL 106). Gradually,

though, it becomes evident that this is a formal gesture of respect in the largest sense. That is, through the nature of the occasion, Derrida incorporates the form of a fundamental attitude that seeks to demonstrate and disseminate all the lessons of temporality, address, unanswerability and responsibility that Levinas's texts themselves have patiently elaborated. It is in this sense, then, a performance of a real philosophical welcoming, which looks to bring out the vital question in Levinas of 'the acceptation of reception' (AEL 26). The heart of Derrida's actual lecture therefore also focuses logically on the key attitudes and potential of hospitality in Levinas, where that word already suggests being both a host and a guest (AEL 36), or a hoster and a hostage (AEL 57). And in a manner that is surely correct on every level, it is only through recognition of and gratitude for the hospitality of Levinas's texts, which Derrida acknowledges through devoted reading of them, that Derrida *then* permits himself to raise quite fundamental questions which arise from the texts' own rigorous teaching.

These questions concern, for example, the central and intractable issues of the necessary but impossible relationship 'between an *ethics* of hospitality (an ethics *as* hospitality) and a *law* or a *politics* of hospitality' (AEL 19), a question whose answer cannot just be deduced from Levinas's discourse, or exhausted by examination (AEL 39). In an extension of this idea concerning politics, Derrida also insists on asking what exactly becomes of the welcome, when the host *becomes* hostage, and whether such a reversion precedes or not the welcoming that is all the same, according to Levinas, originary (AEL 58–59). And then, advancing even further into the tense area of the ethics and politics of the State of Israel, Derrida does not shy away from mentioning how, in 'Politics After!', we are given an irreducible but also problematic relation operating between the interpretation of Zionist commitment and the conception of a peace that would not be purely political (AEL 79). This movement then obliges Derrida to record all the same that he personally does not 'always' endorse 'any of these analyses of the actual situation of the State of Israel in its political visibility' (AEL 79), and that he awaits in both hope and despair for the political invention of Israel to come (AEL 81–82). Another of Derrida's agonistic questions at this point, on sexual difference (AEL 45), is also, as we shall see, taken up explicitly elsewhere by Tina Chanter. So ultimately, what Derrida produces here is an ethically sustained discourse (which he notes even must include silence (AEL 114)) that is marked by both an 'adieu' and a 'welcome', that is to say, is both a greeting and a farewell. Derrida shows then, how it is possible to elaborate a greeting of Levinas's commanding lesson which is nonetheless also able to be properly and thoughtfully a farewell (and, indeed, a benediction: à-Dieu). His text therefore performs for us, in an exemplary and moving way, the obligation that Levinas bequeaths us, which is to learn to give, over the course of a lifetime, a fully realized Levinasian reading.

GIVING LEVINAS: JEAN-LUC MARION

The contemporary Catholic theologian and philosopher Jean-Luc Marion has elaborated an involved phenomenological investigation into giving, that is to say into the nature of donation, or the giving and givenness that exists beyond any compulsion or order. He has furthermore sought to convey how phenomena are saturated with an excess of meaning and the incomprehensibility of the Infinite. More specifically, Marion's readings of Levinas are currently the most ambitious theologically inspired developments of the radical nature of language or figurality in Levinas's work. A good example of this is the key chapter, 'Concerning the Flesh, and Its Arousal', of Marion's 2003 book *The Erotic Phenomenon*, a work completing the trilogy that includes *The Idol and Distance* (1977) and *Prolegomena to Charity* (1986). Here Marion nowhere mentions Levinas since he everywhere incorporates his influence, from the opening considerations of an erotic 'Here I am' (EP 106) through a presentation of the lover's passivity (EP 110), the other's flesh and the caress (EP 120) and the ambiguities of the eroticized face (EP 126) to the phenomena of erotic temporality, finitude and speech. The context in itself not only issues its own highly charged challenge to a prurient reading of Levinas, but also shakes ontology with its intense investigation of love.

Key to Marion's approach, including in the example above, is the notion of appeal, which he raises among other places in a 1996 essay, entitled 'The Voice without Name: Homage to Levinas', that subsequently informed his major work *Being Given: Towards a Phenomenology of Givenness*, published the following year. Following on from the ways in which we move from the ego to the object in Levinas, and the manner in which the face is radically non-visible in his work, Marion regards the *appeal* as the most important innovation that Levinas introduced into phenomenology. With this notion of appeal, Marion seeks to understand how the face, which does not give itself to be simply seen in Levinas, can therefore come to me at all. Marion's answer is that the face's 'self-showing' is achieved phenomenologically through 'self-giving' (VN 225). In Levinas, he sees this occurring through the appeal that addresses me in the face of the Other. Marion radicalizes this self-giving by stressing that the appeal is moreover fundamentally anonymous. In other words, the appeal functions in order not to name itself but to enable the respondent to respond and so become the devotee.

It is here that Marion gives a genial and moving re-reading of the sometimes challenged images of paternity and the child in Levinas. Paternity would seem to contradict the idea of an appeal without name, since a father traditionally and socially gives a proper name to his offspring. But whereas the child is obviously born naturally of the mother, 'strictly speaking he or she is born of an unknown father. The father only finds the child' (VN 236). Paternity is therefore achieved symbolically rather than biologically. The father is therefore only defined as a father by the appeal to recognize his paternity which comes from the infant: '[t]he infant calls silently to the father to give the child his name' (VN 236). And similarly, we can say that there is an appeal from the father in this naming, for the child to accept the burden of the name which names the father as a father. This is anonymous giving, or givenness as such. What is most valuable here is that this theologically inspired reading of a key pathos in Levinas's work opens up the text again at just the moment where other readings, including my own given earlier, have seen a limitation and have become critically distanced. There is a sense in which Marion suggests this metacritical level near the end of *The Erotic Phenomenon* when the child makes a somewhat problematic appearance, noting how in the child's absence, 'I lose not so much the child (who never stops finding and re-finding himself) as I do myself – or rather, ourselves' (EP 206). That is, the child here resembles the third party of justice which Levinas's mature philosophy worked towards. Here Marion's appreciation of Levinas therefore manages in turn to generate a model of critical givenness. In this, it is both consonant with the most advanced attempts on the part of Levinas himself, and a lesson in sustaining and extending an ethical reading.

FEMININE LEVINAS: TINA CHANTER

The position of the feminine in the above theological appreciation is obviously not foregrounded. In a sustained close reading of Levinas with Heidegger, Tina Chanter's 2001 book *Time, Death, and the Feminine* could be said to redress this imbalance, and in the process to set a high standard for feminist reading in general. Chanter notes Derrida's deferment of a choice between two ways of reading Levinas, in *Adieu*, which we indicated earlier: a feminist reading, and another that ignores the androcentrism of Levinas's presentation of femininity. She quotes the precise moment when Derrida decides not to decide: "'Need one choose here between two incompatible readings, between an androcentric hyperbole and a feminist one? Is there a place for such a choice in ethics? And in justice? In law? In politics? Nothing is less certain." (*Adieu* 44)' (TDF 60). It is fair to add right away that Derrida had already pursued the question in 'At This Very Moment in This Work Here I Am', as we noted at the end of our earlier reading of *Otherwise than Being*. Returning to this version of determined uncertainty in her own conclusion, Chanter works through the significance that the feminine acquires in Levinas's contrapuntal depictions of an alternative to an implicitly virile being-unto-death, uncovering in the process the 'sexual specificity' that is a core 'structuring theme of Levinas's discourse' (TDF 250). A genealogy gradually emerges for the 'problem of the feminine' (TDF 254), in Chanter's eyes. There will be a textual movement, facilitated by the feminine, that is resolved or closed by paternity. In addition, the feminine will function structurally as the exception or breakdown or interruption or withdrawal of functionality which, however ethically presented, leaves the feminine as 'that which defies comprehension' (TDF 255). The feminine will also act as the preliminary or sketched or implicit stage on the way to a radicality whose import will nonetheless lead to the overlooking of the feminine as such. Seeking, in spite of these conclusions, to work with the diachrony and plurality of Levinas's account, rather than with abrupt rejection, Chanter views the feminine trope in Levinas via *both* an 'infinitely generous' reading of the feminine projection as the hesitation between saying and said, vulnerability and responsibility, *and* a 'less generously' disposed reading that sees the feminine entrusted with an initial interruption 'but only for the higher purpose of the properly transcendent masculine relationship that it initiates' (TDF 260). Notwithstanding Marion's re-reading, reviewed above, of the function of paternity and the child, Chanter's insightful double reading, with its scrupulous attention to the dynamics of the text, performs here precisely the ethics of reading which Levinas looks in principle to encourage, even if the result does not endorse his writing at every point. In the process, Chanter gives a form of feminism with and through Levinas which shows convincingly how nothing in Levinas is frankly less certain than the simplicity of a relationship between *sexual* politics and ethics.

REVOLUTIONARY LEVINAS: ALAIN BADIOU

Alain Badiou asserts a very different relationship between politics and ethics based on Levinas's work. His *Ethics. An Essay on the Understanding of Evil,* originally published in 1993, and re-issued in 2003 with a new preface, takes the form of an often deliberately irritated dismissal of what in Badiou's view 'Levinas' represents to a certain politics. In typically combative mood, Badiou claims that the term 'ethics' relates these days to human rights by dint of the collapse of revolutionary Marxism. He sets up a dichotomy with 1960s anti-humanism, which Levinas had certainly criticized, somewhat incidentally but consistently. From this position, Badiou reviews contemporary ethical concerns critically: they are (merely) Kantian, overly focused on evil and constantly elaborating victimology. As a result, 'ethics prevents itself from thinking the singularity of situations as such, which is the obligatory starting point of all properly human action' (E 14). This is just a misrepresentation of Levinas's elaboration of ethics, but it serves Badiou's purpose. He can now knock down the ideological framework of ethics which he has himself erected: he asserts, therefore, that Man should be identified only by his affirmative thought, that Evil should be seen to derive from our capability for Good, and not vice versa, and that only singular situations and their possibilities exist, not ethics in general. In fleshing these claims out, he targets Levinas, or rather *Totality and Infinity,* as the origin of the 'ethics of difference' (E 18), even as he cynically acknowledges that 'the contemporary catechism of goodwill [*de la bonne volonté*] with regard to "other cultures", is strikingly [*singulièrement*] distant from Levinas's actual conception [*des conceptions véritables*] of things' (E 20). He characterizes the 'Other' in fact as the *annulment* of philosophy by a theology that itself is no

longer a theology but just 'a dog's dinner' [*de la bouillie pour les chats*]
that has been dished up to replace the former class struggle [*à feu la
lutte des classes*] (E 23). He adds critically that this is a theology that is
also politically and racially integrationist (a criticism that itself raises
serious questions). Following this, Badiou then rapidly states that
infinite alterity is quite simply *what there is*, that thought is not interested in 'culturalism', and that ethics as such does not in fact exist.
Instead, there is only the *ethic-of*, that is to say, the ethic *of* politics, of
love, of science, of art (E 28). Insisting on the irreducible singularities
of this *ethic-of*, Badiou very provocatively takes the limit-case of
Nazism as an example, since it was apparently a simulacrum and as
such represented 'the simulacrum's subversion of the true event' (E
76) and of the sole Good, which is the truth-process (E 87). His
conclusion to this attack is that ethics, or as he now calls it '"ethical"
ideology', is actually the chief adversary of those who are striving to
hold fast to a true thought, and represents the enemy of the impera-
tive to 'Keep going! [*Continuer*]' which belongs to the ethic of truths
(E 67). On one level, this seems an honestly aggressive confrontation
of political positions that claim moral exceptionality in order to evade
answerability. It is all the same a merely political gesture to accuse
Levinas, the philosopher of infinite answerability, of such a ruse.
Badiou's tough assertions also seem to contain the fundamental paradox that, by their very nature, as well as in terms of their reiterated
loyalties and sometimes deliberately excessive language and characterizations, they are actually themselves essentially a moral injunction.
They are disturbingly non-democratic in their (Maoist) appeal to eli-
tist, faceless and ontological processes, and instrumentalist view of
violence in even its most extreme forms. This necessarily creates core
problems for notions of subject potential and thus for agency. Finally,
one can note that Badiou's rejection of a religious apprehension
(whose characterization here tallies not with Levinas but with
Kierkegaard) seems to conflict with both the inherently subjective
nature of the situational reality in Badiou and the resolute determination which the Badiou subject is asked to show. In other words,
Badiou's rejection of consensualism or communitarianism, which he
attributes too hastily as political positions to Levinas, in favour of a
process of extreme singularity that is faithful to the revelations of a
Truth, sounds itself pretty messianic. In sum, a highly overdetermined
'Levinas' is here set up and knocked down by a distinct and unabashed

'ethics'. Perhaps understandably, Badiou is therefore not able to develop a potentially more devastating charge, regarding how Levinas overdetermines Heidegger. Notwithstanding all this, the core virtue of Badiou's forcefulness is perhaps that it blows away all sanctimony and encourages a 'continuing' cross-examination of all political positions and motivations supporting ethical explanations, including by Levinas and 'Levinasians'.

VULNERABLE LEVINAS: JUDITH BUTLER

Political positions and motivations are discernible when Levinas makes a rather dramatic appearance in the final chapter of Judith Butler's 2004 *Precarious Life. The Powers of Mourning and Violence.* Butler's recent work has been described as an 'anti-Badiou manifesto' (N 137). Her context here is the United States' political discourse and policy following the aerial attacks on the Manhattan Twin Towers on 11 September 2001. Levinas's appearance at all on one level is surprising, given the way in which Butler had once described Levinasian positions, in an article entitled 'Ethical Ambivalence', as fetid and masochistic. But on another level, the appearance is perhaps understandable. Judith Butler's analyses of heteronormativity have appealed to the potential of insurrectionary speech and discursive agency, in arguing that 'remainder' subjectivities are produced as abjected by-products of a dynamic that guards normative identities. This ethico-political project, concerning a discursively maintained 'outside' and its ethical disruption, can bear general comparison with Levinas's appreciation of language, ontological closure and ethical dislocation; while its sustaining dimensions of victimology, messianism and internal re-orientation (with attendant calls for justice and social transformation, or presentations of 'subjectivation' and indeed 'subjection') can recall a certain 'Levinas'. *Precarious Life* is composed of five essays written 'in response to the conditions of heightened vulnerability and aggression' (PL xi) that followed the 11 September attacks, and argues in the face of contemporary knee-jerk reaction that 'final control is not, cannot be, an ultimate value' (PL xiii). Instead, we must nurture a provisional collective ethics and politics of resistance based on our shared vulnerability to violence: the precariousness of life. Mechanisms such as obituary writing are identified as a means to determine what is a 'mournable' or 'livable' life, who is ultimately included in the discourse of humanity and how dehumanization can be inflicted. Here Butler introduces Levinas, and specifically the concept of the *face*, taken from *Totality and Infinity*:

> [h]e makes use of the 'face' as a figure that communicates both the precariousness of life and the interdiction on violence ... Although his theological view conjures a scene between two humans each of which bears a face that delivers an ethical demand from a seemingly divine source, his view is nevertheless useful for those cultural analyses that seek to understand how best to depict the human ... Through a cultural transposition of his philosophy, it is possible to see how dominant forms of representation can and must be disrupted.
>
> (PL xviii)

Unfortunately, the *face* is here all too rapidly thematized and recuperated. There is an embarrassed secularization and politicization of theological premises, in the name of cultural transposition, though whose culture and what cultures are questions not posed. Most awkwardly, Butler would presumably characterize the transposing culture as one fundamentally opposing effacement or appropriation; yet in relation to the exceptional nature of the *face* in Levinas, this is what here occurs. The *face* becomes immigrated into an envisaged 'ethic of Jewish non-violence', where 'Jewish' moreover is immediately linked to 'those of us supporting the emergent moment of post-Zionism within Judaism' (PL 140). It is not at all obvious that Levinas would endorse such a position or, more fundamentally, that the textual origins bear such a reduction without experiencing violence. The *face* also here becomes naturalized into a slightly obsessive and frankly banal narrative involving Donald Rumsfeld, the President of Harvard and the *New York Times*, which Levinas might challenge as ultimately evincing mere reciprocal recognition. So the *face* comes to front an increasingly entrapped commentary on media projection or effacement, with an ultimately superfluous use of Levinas that is doubly contradictory, given Butler's concerns about image use and the unappropriable nature of the *face* in *Totality and Infinity*. Given the intelligence and ethical commitment of Butler's text, this is more than simple misappropriation, of course. It is a lesson in itself, both about the profound and detailed problems inherent in the conjunction of ethics and politics in Levinas, as we saw borne out in Levinas's own work, and about the genuine difficulties there are in trying not to generate a thematic and decontextualized incorporation of some of Levinas's most evocative or resonant creations. While *Precarious Life* appeals to a sense of justice and humanity, and a need to safeguard freedoms, then, it also demonstrates the contradictory positions that can be generated if we calculatedly opt for a selective or sentimental use of Levinas.

VIOLENT LEVINAS: SLAVOJ ŽIŽEK

It was the Slovenian-born cultural theorist Slavoj Žižek who referred to Butler's 'ethics of finitude' as anti-Badiou. In the course of reading a German version of her 2003 *Giving an Account of Oneself*, and continuing a debate developed in the 2000 *Contingency, Hegemony, Universality. Contemporary Dialogues on the Left*, Žižek slates Butler for 'making a virtue out of our very weakness' (N 137). This forms a negative basis for his own analysis of Levinas's *face*, given in the 2005 essay 'Neighbors and Other Monsters: A Plea for Ethical Violence', which is collected in *The Neighbor. Three Inquiries in Political Theology*. Typically, the essay borrows formulations from the French psychoanalyst Jacques Lacan, cites popular films as philosophical illustrations, regurgitates earlier publications and slides from one equation to the next (such that Butler somehow morphs into a German-language, anti-Nietzschean, conservative Hegelian, Adorno stand-in) all of which supposedly demonstrates a 'much stronger' approach. Strength here seems to mean calculated belligerence, as borne out in the attention-grabbing title of the section that introduces Levinas: 'Smashing the Neighbor's Face'.

Drawing in almost every case only on Levinas's *Difficult Freedom*, Žižek's essay argues that a critique of ethical violence ignores the violent imposition of divine law at the heart of Jewish tradition, which he claims is needed precisely in order to cover the even more fundamental violence of encountering a neighbour (N 140). Reconfiguring the notion of neighbour straightaway in psychoanalytic terms, so that social neighbourliness merely hides the 'unfathomable abyss of radical Otherness, of a monstrous Thing' (N 143), Žižek therefore states that Levinas's *face* is a case of 'fetishist disavowal' that seeks to gentrify this terrifying Thing (N 146). He eventually further states that what the face-to-face relationship therefore excludes in Levinas is not really the non-European (adding, in a predictable provocation, that 'one is tempted to admire Levinas's readiness to openly admit his being perplexed by the African-Asian other who is too alien to be a neighbor') so much as 'the *inhuman* itself' (N 158), an exclusion that Žižek moreover locates at the heart of Enlightenment dialectics.

At this point, Žižek then introduces in quick succession the *Muselmann* and the *Odradek*. The *Muselmann* is a term borrowed from the writings of concentration camp survivor Primo Levi, by way of the contemporary Italian philosopher Agamben, and was used by camp inmates to denote those who had evidently already lost the will to live, and resembled the living dead. The term *Odradek* comes from the short story 'The Cares of a Family Man' by the Czech-born writer Franz Kafka, by way of its Lacanian interpretation at the hands of the contemporary linguist Jean-Claude Milner, and names a stubborn, minimal entity or presence that resists all attempts by the narrator (or reader) to classify or understand it. Žižek claims that both these figures, in their 'monstrosity' and 'faceless' denial of epiphany or empathy, signal Levinas's 'limitation', exposing the merely 'gentrified' and 'domesticated' nature of his concept of *face* (N 161). The immediately obvious paradox here, however, is that Levinas's supposed domestication of monstrosity through gentrified figurality is a gesture that is at once repeated by Žižek himself, in the way he both introduces and uses the *Muselmann* and the *Odradek*. It is notable how, in contrast to his otherwise carefully populist lures (the *Alien* films, *The Truman Show*, etc.), both figures here are literary, modernist, resonant with specifically European Jewish significance and immediately conceptualized in Lacanian and anti-Levinasian terms. Moreover, if 'the face is the ultimate ethical lure' (N 185), then the domestication of Levinas's presentation of the *face* which Žižek carries out is presumably no less so.

In reality, Žižek seems to be entertaining a disagreement with Butler more than with Levinas. This would explain Žižek's presentation of the face as a mechanism of exclusion, the assertion that 'justice begins when I remember the faceless' (N 182), that is to say, when we get '*beyond* the face of the other', and his presentation of all this as a 'radical anti-Levinasian conclusion' (N 183). These views really derive from a disagreement with Butler and not with Levinas, whom Žižek seems to have not much read. As a result, it is ironically Levinas's accounts that seem the stronger. Žižek's description of the Odradek rather weakly resembles Levinas's horror-filled evocations of the *there is*. Žižek's presentations of the face as a limitation are directly contradicted by Levinas's immediate stress, in *Totality and Infinity*, on how the face 'is present in its refusal to be contained' and 'remains absolute within the relation' (TI 194–95). Žižek's view that we should consider justice in contrast to love (N 182) is anticipated and overtaken by Levinas's conclusions to *Totality and Infinity*, which emphasize how the face, far from establishing co-existence, introduces the 'third party' i.e. justice, so that 'the personal relation is in the rigor of justice which judges me and not in love that excuses me' (TI 304). The most significant omission in Žižek is of any consideration of *Otherwise than Being*, where the face is presented as preceding every pact or consent (OB 88), and where proximity precisely opens up an abyss (OB 93) since it 'already presupposes' justice (OB 157). Given Levinas's actual presentation, then, of the face's 'non-phenomenality' (OB 89), it is Žižek's figures which emerge as limited, local and merely political, while his supposedly anti-Levinasian conclusion, in which the third party's presence suspends the hold of the face (N 183), resembles a timid version of Levinas's developed description of the introduction of justice, where '[t]he relationship with the third party is an incessant correction of the asymmetry of proximity in which the face is looked at' (OB 158). The 'radical negativity' of Žižek's approach has the general beneficial effect of challenging limits to philosophical transcendentalism and political universalism. In pursuing this aim here in relation to 'Levinas', however, Žižek's 'revolutionary justice' (N 186) is arguably actually outdone by the de-localized violence and radicality inherent in Levinas's full presentation of ethics. At the same time, Levinas's conclusion to *Otherwise than Being* could be also read by Žižek. For while reaffirming the unconditionality of being-for-the-other, Levinas adds that a certain weakness, that is to say a 'relaxation of virility without cowardice', is also needed, in support of 'the little humanity' and in repudiation of 'the little cruelty' (OB 185).

These recent critical performances, which represent an advanced ability to take on Levinas, in both senses of the phrase, may in themselves display widely diverging and even conflicting positions. But they all have one critical feature in common: they accept the ethical and analytic value of those questions that keep open the asymmetrical nature of being. As difficult and yet exemplary practices, Levinas's critics can in turn encourage us to challenge and re-formulate an ethics of ethics. And they certainly testify impressively to the continuing relevance and insistent force of the work of Emmanuel Levinas in real critical thought today.

FURTHER READING

A detailed if necessarily incomplete bibliography of works by and on Levinas can be found in: Roger Burggraeve, *Emmanuel Levinas. Une bibliographie primaire et secondaire (1929–1985)* (Leuven: the Centre for Metaphysics and Philosophy of God, 1986).

WORKS BY EMMANUEL LEVINAS

— (1995 [1930/1994]) *The Theory of Intuition in Husserl's Phenomenology*, trans. A. Orianne, Evanston, IL: Northwestern University Press.

Levinas's original thesis and first book-length publication, discussed in chapter 2 of 'Key Ideas'. The work progresses through Husserl's criticism of naturalism, the embedding of science in consciousness, intentionality, the objectifying act and intuition, before raising certain criticisms regarding Husserl's notion of consciousness.

— (1996 [1932]) 'Martin Heidegger and Ontology', trans. Committee of Public Safety, *Diacritics* 26(1), Spring 1996: 11–32.

An early, enthusiastic article on Heidegger, discussed in Chapter 2 of 'Key Ideas', which was originally published in the *Revue philosophique de la France et de l'Etranger*, 53, nos 5–6, May–June 1932; and eventually appeared in a significantly amended version in *En découvrant l'existence avec Husserl et Heidegger*.

— (1990 [1934]) 'Reflections on the Philosophy of Hitlerism', trans. S. Hand, *Critical Inquiry* 17, 63–71.

An astonishingly prescient work, discussed in chapter 2 of 'Key Ideas', which analyses how the philosophy of force inherent in what is identified as Hitlerist philosophy destroys freedom.

———(2003 [1935/1982]) *On Escape*, trans. B. Bergo, Stanford, CA: Stanford University Press.

An early attempt by Levinas, analysed in chapter 2 of 'Key Ideas', to elaborate a philosophy that breaks with totalizing concepts. Its sense of impasse occurs against the backdrop of growing Fascist violence.

— (1988 [1947]) *Existence and Existents*, trans. A. Lingis, Dordrecht, Boston, London: Kluwer.

A book written in part while imprisoned in a Stalag labour camp during the war, and analysed in chapter 2 of 'Key Ideas'. Levinas produces a stark philosophy of survival that contrasts deliberately with the Heideggerian presentation of Being. Contains the centrally important evocation of the *there is*.

— (1987 [1948 (1947)/1979]) *Time and the Other*, trans. R. Cohen, Pittsburgh: Duquesne University Press.

Levinas's post-war lecture series, discussed in chapter 2 of 'Key Ideas', recapitulates and clarifies some of the emerging themes and terms of his philosophy, and looks forward already to aspects of his major work in the sixties. Levinas unambiguously moves beyond Bergson, Sartre and Heidegger in his stronger focus here on the Other.

— (1998 [1949/1967]) *En découvrant l'existence avec Husserl et Heidegger*, partially trans. R. A. Cohen and M. B. Smith as *Discovering Existence with Husserl*, Evanston, IL: Northwestern University Press.

Contains important early essays on Husserl and Heidegger, mentioned in chapter 2 of 'Key Ideas'. Husserl is somewhat recuperated in 1940, while Heidegger is relegated by way of later, critical amendments and omissions made to an original 1932 essay.

— (1969 [1961]) *Totality and Infinity. An Essay on Exteriority*, trans. A. Lingis, Pittsburgh: Duquesne University Press.

The first of Levinas's two most famous texts, which is the subject of chapter 3 of 'Key Ideas'. It represents the most comprehensive critique to this point in Levinas of both Western philosophy's tendency towards totalization, and Levinas's presentation of ethics as first philosophy. The book elevates into a central role the key ethical embodiment of the *face*, as well as bringing in again the themes of enjoyment, the feminine and fecundity which had been sketched in the books of the immediate post-war period.

— (2003 [1972]) *Humanism of the Other*, trans. N. Poller, Urbana and Chicago: University of Illinois Press.

Three essays which oppose aspects of anti-humanist philosophy. The first of these has in mind the work of the German Jewish philosopher Cassirer, who had what became a defining debate with Heidegger at Davos in 1929. The other two, written against the backdrop of May '68, act as a form of appeal by contrasting the then fashionable philosophical notion of the death of the subject being entertained by many students with the genuine authenticity of the students themselves.

— (1996 [1972]) *Proper Names*, trans. M. Smith, London: Athlone.

Contains in fact both the 1975 *Sur Maurice Blanchot* and the 1976 *Noms propres*. Predominantly a collection of mostly brief pieces on writers. The essays on Paul Celan and on Marcel Proust, together with Levinas's important intellectual friendship with Blanchot, are discussed here in chapter 5 of 'Key Ideas'.

— (1998 [1974]) *Otherwise than Being or Beyond Essence*, trans. A. Lingis, Pittsburgh: Duquesne University Press.

The second of Levinas's two most famous works, this is the subject of chapter 4 of 'Key Ideas'. The work challenges even the premises of Levinas's earlier *Totality and Infinity*. In seeking to generate a radical de-thematization of philosophy, it moves away from many of the earlier text's key terms, such as Same or Totality, towards a new set of extreme descriptions, including obsession, hostage and subjection. The important notion of substitution is central to the work.

— (1990 [1963/1976]) *Difficult Freedom*, trans. S. Hand, London: Athlone.

Three decades of articles concerned with Judaism and often touching on the complex questions for justice in Levinas's writings arising from the existence of the State of Israel. Increasingly recognized as indispensable to a full view of Levinas's ideas.

— (1990 [1968 and 1977]) *Nine Talmudic Readings*, trans. A. Aronowicz, Bloomington and Indianapolis: Indiana University Press.

Collects in one English-language volume the 1968 *Quatre lectures talmudiques* and the 1977 *Du sacré au saint*. Discussed in chapter 6 of 'Key Ideas'.

Representative of Levinas's Talmudic readings which he produced annually from the late fifties on.

— (1998 [1982]) *Of God who Comes to Mind*, trans. B. Bergo, Stanford, CA: Stanford University Press.

Essays from the seventies and very early eighties which are all concerned with the notion of 'God' pursued in terms of phenomenological concreteness. Contains the important essay 'God and Philosophy'.

— (1994 [1982]) *Beyond the Verse*, trans. G. D. Mole, Bloomington and Indianapolis: Indiana University Press.

Contains a concluding 'Zionisms' section which is discussed here in chapter 7 of 'Key Ideas'.

— (1985 [1982]) *Ethics and Infinity*, trans. R. Cohen, Pittsburgh: Duquesne University Press.

A series of accessible interviews with Philippe Nemo which covers subjects such as the Bible and philosophy, Heidegger, Love, the Face and the Other. A useful introduction to some of the key concepts.

— (1993 [1987]) *Outside the Subject*, trans. M. B. Smith, London: Athlone.

Fourteen previously uncollected essays, including on Rosenzweig, the Rights of Man and Leiris, the last of which is discussed in chapter 5 of 'Key Ideas'.

— (1987) *Collected Philosophical Papers*, trans. A. Lingis, Dordrecht, Boston, London: Kluwer.

A collection of 11 essays, some of which exist in the volumes above, but which also includes 'Reality and its Shadow', discussed in chapter 5 of 'Key Ideas', and 'Freedom and Command', discussed in chapter 7 of 'Key Ideas'.

— (1994 [1988]) *In the Time of Nations*, trans. M. B. Smith, Bloomington and Indianapolis: Indiana University Press.

Five Talmudic readings given to the annual colloquium of French-speaking Jewish intellectuals in the eighties, and supplemented with essays touching on some aspects of Judaism and exegesis.

— (1989) *The Levinas Reader*, ed. Seán Hand, Oxford: Blackwell.

An edited and introduced collection of representative and often key extracts from Levinas, over a 50-year period.

— (1998 [1991]) *Entre Nous. On Thinking-of-the-Other*, trans. M. B. Smith and B. Harshav, London: Athlone.

Previously uncollected essays and interviews from the fifties on. Includes the early post-war 'Is Ontology Fundamental?'

—— (2000 [1993]) *God, Death, and Time*, trans. B. Bergo, Stanford, CA: Stanford University Press.

Transcripts of two lecture courses delivered in 1975–76, Levinas's final year of teaching at the Sorbonne.

—— (2004 [1994]) *Unforeseen History*, trans. N. Poller, Urbana and Chicago: University of Illinois Press.

A useful collection of pieces that include the early appreciations of Husserl and Heidegger that are discussed in chapter 2, and some of the essays of the fifties and sixties that are discussed in chapter 7 of 'Key Ideas'.

—— (1999 [1995]) *Alterity and Transcendence*, trans. M. B. Smith, London: Athlone.

A collection of ten essays and two interviews written between 1967 and 1989, which all present the idea that transcendence lives in relation to the other.

—— (1999 [1996]) *New Talmudic Readings*, trans. R. A. Cohen, Pittsburgh: Duquesne University Press.

Three Talmudic readings from the seventies and eighties.

—— (2001) *Is it Righteous to Be? Interviews with Emmanuel Levinas*, ed. J. Robbins, Stanford, CA: Stanford University Press.

A clear, useful and comprehensive collection of interviews and discussions from the eighties and nineties.

WORKS ON EMMANUEL LEVINAS

Badiou, A. (2001) *Ethics. An Essay on the Understanding of Evil*, trans. P. Hallward, London and New York: Verso.

A robustly critical view of Levinas, which is discussed in detail in the 'After Levinas' chapter of this book.

Batnitzky, L. (2006) *Leo Strauss and Emmanuel Levinas. Philosophy and the Politics of Revelation*, Cambridge: Cambridge University Press.

A substantial and provocative comparison of these two seemingly very different intellectuals, which seeks to demonstrate their common philosophical sources and parallel thinking, and in this way to pose questions about how religion can make claims on both philosophy and politics.

Bergo, B. (1999) *Levinas between Ethics and Politics. For the Beauty that Adorns the Earth*, Dordrecht and London: Kluwer.

Principally concerned with the relations between ethics and justice in Levinas's philosophy. The second part of the work develops its own criticisms regarding what the Levinasian 'ought' is grounded in, and in what sense it is exceptional.

Bernasconi, R. and S. Critchley (eds) (1991) *Re-reading Levinas*, London: Athlone.

An early but still essential collection that includes translations of Levinas's 'Wholly Otherwise' and Derrida's 'At This Vvery Moment in This Work Here I am', plus – among others – Luce Irigaray's 'Questions to Emmanuel Levinas', Tina Chanter's 'Antigone's Dilemma' and Bernasconi's essay on scepticism. Reprints Critchley's '"Bois" – Derrida's Final Word on Levinas' which formed the third chapter of his 1992 book listed below.

Bernasconi, R. and S. Critchley (eds) (2002) *The Cambridge Companion to Levinas*, Cambridge: Cambridge University Press.

Contains several important commentators, such as Putnam, Chalier, Llewelyn, Wyschogrod and Bernasconi. Bernet's essay on Levinas's critique of Husserl is valuable, as is Stella Sandford's analysis of the status of the feminine in Levinas.

Bernasconi, R. and D. Wood (eds) (1988) *The Provocation of Levinas. Rethinking the Other*, London and New York: Routledge.

A strong collection of dialogic essays, featuring Tina Chanter (on 'Feminism and the Other'), Christina Howells (on Sartre and Levinas) and Bernasconi (on Buber and Levinas), and including a translation of Levinas's 1982 'Useless Suffering'.

Bloechl, T. (ed.) (2000) *The Face of the Other and the Trace of God. Essays on the Philosophy of Emmanuel Levinas*, New York: Fordham University Press.

Twelve essays equally divided between an examination of how Levinas's thought intersects with that of other philosophers such as Husserl, Kierkegaard and Sartre, and of key theological questions. Includes the Marion essay listed here below and discussed in the 'After Levinas' chapter of this book.

Caygill, H. (2002) *Levinas and the Political*, London and New York: Routledge.

A strong analysis, in clear and detailed prose, of the inherently political nature of all of Levinas's writing. Gives welcome attention to some of the incidental essays, arguing powerfully how these can elucidate the major works and indeed underpin the larger ethical generalizations.

Chalier, C. (1982) *Figures du féminin. Lectures d'Emmanuel Levinas*, Paris: La Nuit surveillée.

Looks sympathetically at metaphorical women, female exteriority and the feminine aspects of language in Levinas.

Chanter, T. (2001) *Time, Death, and the Feminine. Levinas with Heidegger*, Stanford, CA: Stanford University Press.

A powerful, detailed and persuasive work which is discussed in the chapter 'After Levinas' in this book.

Cohen R. A. (ed.) (1986) *Face to Face with Levinas*, Albany: State University of New York Press.

Includes translations of Blanchot's 'Our Clandestine Companion', Lyotard's 'Levinas's Logic' and Irigaray's 'The Fecundity of the Caress', in addition to good essays by Peperzak (on Hegel, Kant and Levinas) and Alphonso Lingis (on the Sensuality and the Sensitivity).

Critchley, S. (1992) *The Ethics of Deconstruction. Derrida and Levinas*, Oxford: Blackwell.

A now early but still essential presentation of the implications for deconstruction of Levinas's ethics, focusing in particular on the discursive relation established between Levinas and Derrida.

Davies, C. (1996) *Emmanuel Levinas. An Introduction*, Oxford and Cambridge: Polity.

A clear and accurate guide that focuses on phenomenology and the central texts *Totality and Infinity* and *Otherwise than Being*, but also considers some of the Talmudic readings and *Difficult Freedom* under the rubric of 'Religion'.

Derrida, J. (1978 [1967]) 'Violence and Metaphysics: An Essay on the Thought of Emmanuel Levinas', in *Writing and Difference*, trans. A. Bass, London and Henley: Routledge and Kegan Paul, pp. 79–153.

One of the key early moments of reception of Levinas, which introduced Levinas to a wider audience and arguably set the terms for Levinas's own future work. Discussed in chapter 3 of 'Key Ideas'.

Derrida, J. (1991 [1980]) 'At This Very Moment in This Work Here I Am', trans. R. Berezdivin, in *Re-reading Levinas*, eds R. Bernasconi and S. Critchley, pp. 11–48.

A second key essay from Derrida, which is discussed in chapter 4 of 'Key Ideas'.

Derrida, J. (1999) *Adieu to Emmanuel Levinas*, trans. P.-A. Brault and M. Naas, Stanford, CA: Stanford University Press.

Produced in the aftermath of Levinas's death, a respectful, moving and delicately critical account of Levinas's work, which is discussed in detail in this book's chapter 'After Levinas'.

Eaglestone, R. (1997) *Ethical Criticism. Reading after Levinas*, Edinburgh: Edinburgh University Press.

One of the first and still best demonstrations of the centrality of Levinas's ethics to criticism, literary theory and literature. Offers both detailed understanding of Levinas's complex relation to the artwork and a contextualized assessment that draws on other theorists of ethics such as Martha Nussbaum and J. Hillis Miller.

Gibbs, R. (1992) *Correlations in Rosenzweig and Levinas*, Princeton, NJ: Princeton University Press.

Draws out the basic affinities linking these two seemingly different philosophers, with valuable chapters on speech as performance as well as tensions between politics and aesthetics. Also includes useful comparisons with Hermann Cohen and Gabriel Marcel, and a final insightful chapter on Marx and Levinas.

Hand, S. (ed.) (1996) *Facing the Other. the Ethics of Emmanuel Levinas*, London: RoutledgeCurzon.

Nine new critical essays combining a wide variety of approaches to Levinas, including from the perspectives of psychoanalysis, Jewish studies, philosophy, literary criticism, feminism and theology.

Handelman, S. (1991) *Fragments of Redemption. Jewish Thought and Literary Theory in Benjamin, Scholem, and Levinas*, Bloomington and Indianapolis: Indiana University Press.

A still valuable work that places Levinas in the context of the other writers and describes key themes, approaches to Talmudic reading, forms of philosophical saying and notions of messianism.

Hutchens, B. C. (2004) *Levinas. A Guide for the Perplexed*, New York and London: Continuum.

A knowledgeable and closely written thematic guide to some of the key notions in Levinas's philosophy.

Katz, C. E. (2003) *Levinas, Judaism, and the Feminine. The Silent Footsteps of Rebecca*, Bloomington and Indianapolis: Indiana University Press.

Presents positively the links between the feminine and religion in Levinas's work. Contests the view that women or maternity are essentialist in Levinas.

Keenan, D. K. (1999) *Death and Responsibility. The "Work" of Levinas*, Albany: State University of New York Press.
Argues in a tightly organized book that the general notion of responsibility in Levinas's ethics is actually strongly dependent on his accounts of death.

Laruelle, F. (1980) *Textes pour Emmanuel Levinas*, Paris: J-M Place.
Includes the French text of Derrida's 'At This Very Moment', as well as Ricœur's 'L'Originaire de la question-en-retour dans le *Krisis* de Husserl'.

Lescourret, M.-A. (1994) *Emmanuel Levinas*, Paris: Flammarion.
A generous if uncritical biographical account running up until the production of *Otherwise than Being*.

Llewelyn, J. (2000) *The Hypocritical Imagination. Between Kant and Levinas*, London and New York: Routledge.
A brilliant and challenging work that champions the cause of imagination in the face of certain strictures located in Levinas. In extending the reach of imagination, and the language we can use to describe such an extended reach, Llewelyn gives powerful readings of Schelling, Hegel, Heidegger and Emily Dickinson.

Malka, S. (2002) *Emmanuel Levinas. La vie et la trace*, Paris: J. C. Lattès.
An appreciative general biography of Levinas which draws in part on recollections given by colleagues, friends, family and former students.

Marion, J.-L. (2000) 'The Voice without Name: Homage to Levinas', in *The Face of the Other and the Trace of God. Essays on the Philosophy of Emmanuel Levinas*, ed. T. Bloechl, New York: Fordham University Press, pp. 224–42.
An appreciation by a difficult contemporary theologian, which is discussed in the chapter 'After Levinas'.

Mole, G. D. (1997) *Lévinas, Blanchot, Jabès. Figures of Estrangement*, Gainesville: University Press of Florida.
One of the earliest studies to consider Levinas, Blanchot and Jabès together, from the perspectives of writing and exile, ethics and metaphysics, and the Shoah's repercussions for the possibilities of discourse and the artwork.

Moses, S. (2004) *Au-delà de la guerre. Trois études sur Levinas*, Paris and Tel Aviv: Editions de l'éclat.

Includes consideration of how Rosenzweig, paternity and the infinite are important issues in Levinas.

Moyn, S. (2005) *Origins of the Other. Emmanuel Levinas between Revelation and Ethics*, Ithaca and London: Cornell University Press.

An important work that seeks to counteract what it views as certain prevalent images of Levinas, by focusing most particularly on the earlier years and arguing persuasively that Levinas gradually crafts an idiosyncratic Judaism rather than return to any traditional source.

Peperzak, A. (1993) *To the Other. An Introduction to the Philosophy of Emmanuel Levinas*, West Lafayette, IN: Purdue University Press.

Gives a detailed reading of the essay 'Philosophy and the Idea of the Infinite', plus a clear account of the core themes of *Totality and Infinity*.

Peperzak, A. (ed.) (1995) *Ethics as First Philosophy. The Significance of Emmanuel Levinas for Philosophy, Literature and Religion*, New York and London: Routledge.

Includes many of the essential commentators on Levinas, such as Chalier, Gibbs, Bernasconi, Wyschogrod, Robbins and Llewelyn. Contains a number of valuable comparisons of Levinas's ethical and religious strains, including Peperzak's own essay on 'Transcendence'.

Peperzak, A. (1997) *Beyond. The Philosophy of Emmanuel Levinas*, Evanston, IL: Northwestern University Press.

A series of close and appreciative readings of different aspects of Levinas's thought, ranging from the relationship between Judaism and philosophy through to issues of language and presentation. Includes again the essay on transcendence given in the Peperzak edition of essays listed above.

Poirié, F. (1987) *Emmanuel Lévinas. Qui êtes-vous?*, Paris: La Manufacture.

An early but still useful biography with interviews and extracts. The heart of the text is translated in *Is it Righteous to Be?*

Purcell, M. (2006) *Levinas and Theology*, Cambridge: Cambridge University Press.

A focused presentation of the relationship between Levinas's general ideas and their implications for a fundamental and practical theology. Includes analysis of Levinas's phenomenological theology in the light of Rahner and Marion, as well as discussion of Janicaud's objections.

Robbins, J. (1999) *Altered Reading. Levinas and Literature*, Chicago and London: University of Chicago Press.

A valuable discussion of the status of the literary in the main philosophical texts, as well as of some of Levinas's essays on literature. Traces well the philosophical links in the *there is*, and includes in an appendix a translation of Georges Bataille's review of Levinas's *From Existence to Existents*.

Schroeder, B. (1999) *Altared Ground. Levinas, History, and Violence*, London and New York: Routledge.

An analysis of the various non-totalizing 'grounds' ('Helioground', 'Ideoground', 'Mystiground', etc.) which the author discerns in Levinas's presentation of the ethical relation.

Toumayan, A. (2004) *Encountering the Other. The Artwork and the Problem of Difference in Blanchot and Levinas*, Pittsburgh: Duquesne University Press.

A clear and well-paced analysis of key intersections between the themes and structural solutions of these two thinkers, with a particular focus on the *there is*.

Trezise, T. (ed.) (2004) *Encounters with Levinas* (Yale French Studies 104) New Haven: Yale University Press.

Seven essays combining recent readings (including anticipatory extracts from Moyn and Batnitsky) and recapitulations (Irigaray) or reprints (Ricœur).

Wright, T. (1999) *The Twilight of Jewish Philosophy. Emmanuel Levinas' Ethical Hermeneutics*, Amsterdam: Harwood Academic.

A very clear and helpful guide to the relationship between Levinas's ethical philosophy, as borne out in the two major works, and his understanding of Judaism.

WORKS CITED

Badiou, A. (2001 [1993/2003]) *Ethics. An Essay on the Understanding of Evil*, trans. P. Hallward, London: Verso.

Blanchot, M. (1986 [1980]) *The Writing of the Disaster*, trans. A. Smock, Lincoln and London: University of Nebraska Press.

Butler, J. (2000) 'Ethical Ambivalence', in *The Turn to Ethics*, eds Marjorie Garber, Beatrice Hanssen and Rebecca L. Walkowitz, New York and London: Routledge, pp. 15–28.

Butler, J. (2004) *Precarious Life. The Powers of Mourning and Violence*, London and New York: Verso.

Chanter, T. (2001) *Time, Death, and the Feminine. Levinas with Heidegger*. Stanford, CA: Stanford University Press.

Halperin, J. and G. Levitte (eds) (1976) *La conscience juive face à la guerre. Données et débats*, Paris: Presses Universitaires de France.

Hand, S. (1996) 'Shadowing Ethics: Levinas's View of Art and Aesthetics', in *Facing the Other. The Ethics of Emmanuel Levinas*, ed. S. Hand, London: RoutledgeCurzon, pp. 63–89.

Heidegger, M. (2002 [first delivered 1935, published 1960]) 'The Origin of the Work of Art', trans. A. Hofstadter, in *Martin Heidegger, Basic Writings*, ed. David Farrell Krell, London: Routledge, pp. 143–212.

Heidegger, M. (1987 [1953]) *An Introduction to Metaphysics*, trans. R. Manheim, New Haven and London: Yale University Press.

Heidegger, M. (1996 [1984]) *Hölderlin's Hymn 'The Ister'*, trans. W. McNeill and J. Davis, Bloomington and Indianapolis: Indiana University Press.

Lacoue-Labarthe, Ph. (1990 [1987]) *Heidegger, Art and Politics. The Fiction of the Political*, trans. C. Turner, Oxford: Blackwell.

Marion, J.-L. (2000) 'The Voice without Name: Homage to Levinas', in *The Face of the Other and the Trace of God*, ed. J. Bloechl, New York: Fordham University Press, pp. 224–42.

Marion, J.-L. (2007 [2003]) *The Erotic Phenomenon*, trans. S. E. Lewis, Chicago and London: University of Chicago Press.

Rosenzweig, F. (2002 [1921]) *The Star of Redemption*, trans. W. Hallo, Indiana: University of Notre Dame Press.

Žižek, S. (2005) 'Neighbors and Other Monsters: A Plea for Ethical Violence', in *The Neighbor. Three Inquiries in Political Theology*, eds Slavoj Žižek, Eric L. Santer and Kenneth Reinhard, Chicago and London: University of Chicago Press.

INDEX

Related titles from Routledge

Critical Theory Today

Second Edition

Lois Tyson

This new edition of the classic guide offers a thorough and accessible introduction to contemporary critical theory. It provides in-depth coverage of the most common approaches to literary analysis today: feminism, psychoanalysis, Marxism, reader-response theory, new criticism, structuralism and semiotics, deconstruction, new historicism, cultural criticism, lesbian/gay/queer theory, African-American criticism, and postcolonial criticism.

The chapters provide an extended explanation of each theory, using examples from everyday life, popular culture, and literary texts; a list of specific questions critics who use that theory ask about literary texts; an interpretation of F. Scott Fitzgerald's *The Great Gatsby* through the lens of each theory; a list of questions for further practice to guide readers in applying each theory to different literary works; and a bibliography of primary and secondary works for further reading.

This book can be used as the only text in a course or as a precursor to the study of primary theoretical works. It motivates readers by showing them what critical theory can offer in terms of their practical understanding of literary texts and in terms of their personal understanding of themselves and the world in which they live. Both engaging and rigorous, it is a 'how-to' book for undergraduate and graduate students new to critical theory and for college professors who want to broaden their repertoire of critical approaches to literature.

ISBN 13: 978-0-415-97409-7 (hbk)
ISBN 13: 978-0-415-97410-3 (pbk)

Available at all good bookshops
For ordering and further information please visit:

Fifty Key Literary Theorists

Richard J. Lane

What is it that defines literary theory? Richard J. Lane explores fifty influential figures who have shaped this field over the last century. In one volume, theorists from a multitude of disciplines are brought together in order to explore literary theory in all its diversity, covering feminism to postcolonialism, postmodernism to psychoanalysis.

Each entry deals with key concepts and ideas that have informed literary studies in the twentieth and twenty-first centuries. Included in this comprehensive guide are entries on:

- Roland Barthes
- Judith Butler
- Jacques Derrida
- Sigmund Freud
- Edward W. Said

An essential resource for all students of literature, *Fifty Key Literary Theorists* explores the gamut of critical debate, offering both an excellent introduction to and a comprehensive overview of modern literary theorists.

ISBN13: 978-0-415-33847-9 (hbk)
ISBN13: 978-0-415-33848-6 (pbk)
ISBN13: 978-0-203-44142-8 (ebk)

Literary Theory: The basics

Third Edition

Hans Bertens

With a new introduction and fully updated pointers to further reading, this third edition of Hans Bertens' bestselling book is a must-have guide to the world of literary theory.

Exploring a broad range of topics from Marxist and feminist criticism to post-modernism and new historicism it includes new coverage of:

- the latest developments in post-colonial and cultural theory
- literature and sexuality
- the latest schools of thought, including eco-criticism and post-humanism
- the future of literary theory and criticism.

Literary Theory: The basics is an essential purchase for anyone who wants to know what literary theory is and where it is going.

ISBN13: 978-0-415-39670-7 (hbk)
ISBN13: 978-0-415-39671-4 (pbk)

Available at all good bookshops
For ordering and further information please visit
www.routledgeliterature.com

THE NEW CRITICAL IDIOM

Series Editor: John Drakakis, University of Stirling

The New Critical Idiom is an invaluable series of introductory guides to today's critical terminology. Each book:

- provides a handy, explanatory guide to the use (and abuse) of the term
- offers an original and distinctive overview by a leading literary and cultural critic
- relates the term to the larger field of cultural representation

With a strong emphasis on clarity, lively debate and the widest possible breadth of examples, *The New Critical Idiom* is an indispensable approach to key topics in literary studies.

'*The New Critical Idiom* is a constant resource – essential reading for all students.'

Tom Paulin, *University of Oxford*

'Easily the most informative and wide-ranging series of its kind, so packed with bright ideas that it has become an indispensable resource for students of literature.'

Terry Eagleton, *University of Manchester*

Available in this series:

For further information on individual books in the series, visit:
www.routledgeliterature.com